# UNCHAIN
## Me Mama

### THE FORGIVENESS FACTOR
#### LESSONS LEARNED ON MY
#### JOURNEY TO UNDERSTANDING

*Unchain Me Mama: The Forgiveness Factor*

**Editing**
*Robin R. Ashworth, Ph.D LLC*

**Book Creation & Design**
*DHBonner Virtual Solutions, LLC*
www.dhbonner.net

**ISBN:** 978-1-7323003-7-8

Printed in the United States of America

# UNCHAIN Me Mama

## THE FORGIVENESS FACTOR
### LESSONS LEARNED ON MY
### JOURNEY TO UNDERSTANDING

COMPILED BY

# AUDRA LOWRAY UPCHURCH

## FOREWORD BY ANN M. DILLARD

# Contents

# Foreword

*"If you're not being defined by a vision of the future, then you're left with the old memories of the past and you will be predictable in your life."* ~ Dr. Joe Dispenza

*"We repeat what we don't repair."* ~ Christine Langley-Obaugh

It's Emotional! It's Biological! It's Spiritual! It's Physical! It's Psychological! The mother-daughter relationship is all of these things and so much more! As women, this relationship tends to be the blueprint for all of our other relationships. During the course of the mother-daughter journey, there are circumstances that happen and cause emotional fractures. Without awareness and acknowledgment of these fractures and their causes, they are subject to spiraling into monumental breaks in the relationship.

I am a living example because I have been a great mother AND I made some huge mistakes in raising my children. I watched helplessly as my daughter repeated some of my struggles with emotional eating and weight gain. This caused sadness, pain, hurt, shame, guilt, and embarrassment. I believe that many mothers and daughters can relate to some of these emotions.

As a co-author in the Amazon Bestselling anthology *Unchain My Legacy,* conceived by visionary author, Audra Lowray Up-church, I shared my story about the emotional debt that I inherited from my mother and passed on to my daughter, even though I vowed to never do that. In many communities, this trend is classified as a generational curse. I also shared about repair, restoration, love, hope, grace, and forgiveness. This has been an intensely transparent, vulnerable, yet rewarding process. So many mothers and daughters have expressed their desire to repair their relationships and build stronger bonds, but are unsure of where to start.

Amazon four-time bestselling author, Audra Lowray Upchurch, is an icon among women. She has given scores of women, from all walks of life, the courage and the platform to find their voices and share their stories in her Unchain book series. Audra has provided the platform they need to explore the abuse, hurt, pain, and toxicity of their mother-daughter relationships. Women from all over the country have relished this opportunity to experience freedom that only comes through sharing and deconstructing the complexities of motherhood wounds.

Out of her own story of being a teen mom with very little direction, and significant challenges, Audra has birthed an unchained movement. Her transparency about her motherhood journey, coupled with her authenticity, allows women to easily and deeply connect with Audra. While she is helping women to speak their truth and find emotional freedom, she is also equipping them with the tools to be financially free through entrepreneurship. Being one of Audra's co-authors is more than writing a chapter in one of her books. Her co-authors benefit from her fierce business acumen, generosity, expansive professional network, and tools to be able to execute masterfully.

As one of these women, the unchaining process began for me

with an awareness that being a mother encompasses far more than just being the elder female of the pair. I held the answers and solutions to unresolved generational patterns and by acknowledging this, I could free my daughter. What I did not realize at the time when I started my unchaining process was how differently we experience the same events.

Witnessing and affirming my daughter's truth often left me feeling inadequate as a mother. This is the pain and agony that many mothers try so desperately to avoid, resulting in many daughters never getting the validation and apologies that they need for their healing.

As you read the compelling life stories of the co-authors in this book, you will discover many of them have had to make difficult decisions to redefine their futures because the painful memories of their pasts would only lead to another generation of motherhood hurts. These courageous women chronicled their choices to forge ahead and be in relationship with their mothers, who are unable, unwilling, unavailable, or ill-equipped to help them heal. They have chosen to forgive.

According to Webster's Dictionary, to forgive is "to stop feeling angry or resentful toward someone for an offense, flaw, or mistake. It is to cancel a debt." Forgive is an action word. Forgiveness is a process that must be repeated over and over again. It is not a 'one-and-done' deal. When it comes to the mother-daughter relationship, this is one of the most monumental tasks women must conquer in order to have a healthy relationship.

Once I started this process with my daughter, I also came full circle with my own mother. Like many mothers in her generation, her idea of establishing a close mother-daughter relationship was to "let bygones be bygones" and to "forgive and forget." This is nearly impossible because the very offenses that have been caused by unburdened mothers with their unresolved issues have become a part of their daughters' DNA.

In my own work with my daughter and my mother, as well as working with my clients, the resistance of mothers to acknowledge that they have erred comes from a place of hierarchal superiority and entitlement. This stance says, "I have made so many sacrifices for you and you are being so ungrateful by even bringing up such things, which are really not true."

So often daughters hold their mothers in such high esteem and many times, to unrealistic standards. The realization that mothers and grandmothers have their own trauma histories helps daughters to see their mothers in a more realistic light as flawed human beings. With a deeper, more thorough understanding of our mothers' stories, daughters are enlightened to the fact that what might seem like anger is really fear and a desire to protect their daughters. Love is usually the driving, but unrecognized force behind these messy complexities. It is when these revelations have occurred that daughters are better able to forgive and extend a measure of grace, even when the forgiveness is unsolicited by their mothers.

The alternative to forgiveness is emotional death. Spiritual teacher and author Marianne Williamson writes, "Unforgiveness is like drinking poison yourself and waiting for the other person to die." When we walk in unforgiveness, we subconsciously dim our own light and inadvertently pass on unhealthy, generational patterns to yet another generation, thus perpetuating generational curses.

As you read the riveting stories of these amazing women, you will notice a few things:

- Daughters long for the unconditional love, affirmation, and acceptance of their mothers.
- Forgiveness must happen even when it is not solicited.
- When mothers are unavailable or unwilling to participate in the healing process, there is sometimes a need for surrogacy in the daughter's life, to help meet the need for acceptance and validation.
- As humans, forgiveness is more for the person who is choosing to forgive than it is for the offender.
- The negative impact of the mother-daughter conflict affects all other relationships.
- In some cases, daughters are willing to bear the full burden of the problematic relationship in order to spare their mothers the sadness and grief.
- Mothers are carrying the guilt of their past, which is evident in their relationships with their daughters.
- For mothers to accept responsibility for the trauma that has been passed on to their daughters, they would have to admit their own trauma.
- Forgiveness must not be confused with repair. These are two different parts of the healing journey.
- Forgiveness must be accompanied by the establishment of healthy relational boundaries. Without proper boundaries

in the mother-daughter relationship, either party is subject to more offenses.

As these stories inspire you, I challenge you to examine your own mother-daughter journey. If you are gifted with new awareness, I appeal to you to take the next steps and acknowledge that you, too, have made mistakes as a mother. Give yourself permission to hold both the space of being a good mother and causing hurt to your daughter at the same time. Extend your daughter the gift of acknowledgment and validation. It will free her! It will heal her! It will unchain your future generations!

~ *Ann M. Dillard,* **LMFT**
**Founder of KIP Consulting Services, LLC**
*and* **Mother-Daughter Relationship Healer**

# Introduction:
# Chained by Shame, Unchained by Grace

*By Audra Lowray Upchurch*

*My homeless mother was sleeping on the*
*subway, and I was ashamed.*

I was 15 years old, with my friends, coming home from Washington Irving high school. We had jumped on the A train at the Broadway-Nassau Station and were clowning around having fun, walking from one train car to the next. And then I saw her, and for a moment, time froze. There she was on the train, sleeping and homeless.

I immediately picked up my pace so my friends wouldn't notice – or really so she wouldn't notice – and we kept moving to the next car. My heart was racing, and I could barely hear what my friends were saying because all that kept running through my mind were questions. Is mommy okay? Did she see me? Did anyone notice? And my other thought: I hate my life.

Growing up as the daughter of a woman with mental illness was difficult, to say the least. At a young age, I became accustomed to feeling shame because it seemed a normal part of my life. We were always lacking some basic necessity: food, clothing, and eventually shelter. Once a teacher scolded me because I came to school without a pencil. She looked at me with disdain and asked, "So you want me to believe that you can't afford a ten-cent pencil?" With tears in my eyes, I looked away as the other kids began to laugh. Immediately the teacher knew she'd made a mistake, opened up her desk drawer and handed me a pencil. I wiped my tears and tried to proceed as if nothing had happened. But the kids taunted me the rest of the day. That was my norm. Shame. Embarrassment. Resentment. Not towards my teacher, but towards my mother. I blamed my mother for all of it.

My school years were especially tough because we moved so frequently. Every time I would come out of my shell and start to connect with my teachers and classmates, we'd move...again. I'd have to repeat instances similar to the "pencil incident" over and over. By sixth grade, I had been transferred out of school thirteen times. Our moves were mostly triggered by my mother's erratic job history and unemployment. She would often apply for jobs she couldn't do and be promptly fired, or get a job and leave it due to an imaginary conflict.

As a child, I just wanted to run and hide because I couldn't stop what was going on. I had no control over my mother's actions or their impact on my life. As my mom's mental illness spiraled completely out of control, she began sleeping in the subway and was lost to me, absorbed with her own made-up world.

As I grew into adulthood, that sense of shame, and the fear of discovery didn't leave. I would cringe when on a date and a gentleman would ask about my family. At company events, when my co-workers would reminiscence and share childhood stories, I kept silent. I couldn't escape the sting of these constant reminders that I'd always be the daughter of a woman with mental illness. I simply could not outrun, or out-perform my past, and the shame it always brought.

I allowed the shame I felt about my mother's mental illness to shape how I interacted with others, and how I saw myself. It had me so bound, that some of the choices I made were to my own detriment, and that caused my shame to morph into resentment. Resentment became anger directed squarely at my unhealthy mother. But just as I did when scolded by my teacher, I ignored my pain, wiped my tears and proceeded living my life. I had become completely acclimated to my feelings of shame.

It wasn't until I was in my forties that I began to understand that not only was my mother's mental illness nothing to be ashamed of, but that I could do my part in helping others who were in similar positions. It began with me forgiving her first, and then myself. For me, forgiveness was a layered, labored process. It was difficult, and even ugly at times, but it freed me.

For so many years, I felt guilty about seeing my mom on the train and not stopping to run and hug her. Forgiving my mom opened the door for me to forgive myself. And so I say to you that regardless of how sharp the pain, how deep the shame, forgiveness is always a healing choice open to you.

This is why I feel so strongly compelled to share with you the stories in *Unchain Me Mama: The Forgiveness Factor.* These brave women share not only the very personal challenges and hurts of difficult relationships with their mothers, but also their triumphs, large and small, in learning to forgive it all. As you read these chapters, I hope you find inspiration to begin to forgive your mother. I also hope you can lean on us and find the Grace to forgive yourself.

# Naturally Ever After: Forgiving Through Healthy Living

*By Nydia E. Guity*

*"You got the light, count it all joy*
*You got the right to be mad*
*But when you carry it along, you'd find that only getting in the way*
*They say you have to let it goe."*
*– from 'Mad' by Solange*

*"Apurate! No te lo voy a decir otra vez!"* ("Hurry up! I am not going to tell you again!") My mother called to us in an elevated tone of voice.

It was around 1:00 am and we had just come home from my cousin's birthday party in Far Rock Away in Queens, New York. The trains weren't running on the regular schedule, and so what should have been a one hour and forty-five-minute train ride ended up being close to four hours. And I had to wake up early for school. A day off would have been nice, but in my Garifuna household, perfect attendance was non- negotiable. Since kindergarten, I was one of only a very few to receive the perfect attendance award at the end of the spring semester. Rain, sleet or snow, it didn't matter, my mom was taking me to school.

Reaching home, I remember running up the stairs of our South

1

Bronx, three-bedroom apartment and racing my younger sister to the bathroom. Yes! I said with excitement as I won the race and sat on the toilet to relieve myself after holding my urine on the longest train ride in the history of my nine years of life. My younger sister was banging on the restroom door and whining about how long I was taking.

I quickly rolled toilet tissue around my hands to clean myself and when I drew it back, I saw something I had never seen before: there was blood! With the rolled tissue still on my hand displaying evidence that I was officially a young lady, I pulled my pants up and ran back downstairs yelling *"Mami, Mami mira!"* ("Mom, Mom! Look!").

My mother was organizing the dining room and turned toward me. I remember her fussing at me about how I should be sleeping, but when I waved the tissue in her face, she stopped, and her eyes welled up with tears. My mom hugged me and promptly helped me get cleaned up, then shared her stash of sanitary napkins with me. I thought they looked like incomplete diapers. Still, it was a special moment between us.

My first menstrual cycle lasted about five days and then would periodically come to visit every three to four months. The doctors told my mom this was because I was so young, but as I got older my body would regulate itself. My younger sister, who was fourteen months younger than me, became a young lady shortly after my eleventh birthday, but unlike me, her cycle came to visit every single month like clockwork. My menstrual cycle was irregular for years after my eleventh birthday. That irregularity, which was completely out of my control, would quickly become the catalyst for difficulty between my mother and me.

My mom would say that people who don't have their periods are either pregnant or have menopause and I didn't fall in either category. Pregnant! Me? An 11-year-old, pregnant! Why would she think that of me? Because of her poor and uninformed assumptions, I was often the target of her criticism and judgment.

One summer day I was at the park with my younger sister and brother, I looked at the clock on my giga-pet and my heart started to race. It was 7:55 pm, and I had to make sure we were home by 8 pm, but it was a ten-minute walk back to our apartment.

"Let's go! We have to go home before I get in trouble!" I yelled to my siblings.

I could feel the wind blowing and drops of water coming from the sky. I rolled my eyes at the thought of the verbal lashing I was going to get from my mother for being late again. It never mattered that her other two kids were the ones dragging their feet. Things always seemed to be my fault and I was getting tired of proving my point all of the time. I started to tell my friends that I had to go and started walking home. I turned around and my younger siblings were taking their sweet time walking behind me with their faces pouting in disappointment.

I put the key in the lock and turned it to open the door, as my younger siblings pushed past me and ran upstairs. As I locked the door behind me, my mother and aunt were sitting in the living room and I could feel their eyes on me.

My mother demanded, "didn't you see that it was raining? Why did you wait so long to come home with the kids?"

I felt my jaw clenching. I took a deep breath, and as lightly as I could replied, "It just started to rain and I tried to get them to hurry so that ..."

I was quickly interrupted and told not to talk back. I never understood the purpose of asking a question and then getting upset when I responded. I turned toward the stairs and walked to my bedroom. I could hear my mother talking about the friends I was choosing and how I needed to be careful with the decisions I was making.

It was exactly that kind of scrutiny that drove me crazy. I started to sweat, and my face was scorching. I wanted to leave but had nowhere to go. I thought to myself, I do everything that she asks. I help with my younger siblings, I do well in school and have had perfect attendance for all of my life. My mom was the kind of parent who monitored my every move and when she was not around her friends in our neighborhood would watch me and report to her if they noticed any concerns. There were always eyes on me, so where would I have the time to even meet a boy, let alone make a baby?

I was four minutes late! I thought to myself, *in seven years, I'll be eighteen and I can't wait to just get away from her!*

Finally, in my bedroom, I closed the door behind me and flopped on my bed to look out the window. I slid off my all-white K-Swiss sneakers, buried my head between my legs, and just sobbed. I was a bit embarrassed, but mostly I was consumed with anger. I could hear the six train ease into the station on Whitlock Ave as raindrops began to hit my window with force as the wind blew stronger and stronger. The weather reflected how I felt most days.

I was the oldest of three children with responsibilities that I did not want. Everything always seemed to be my fault, and even when I tried to explain it didn't matter.

Despite my bedroom door being closed, I could still hear my mother talking about me. I hated when she talked about me and my friends. My friends were not angels, but they weren't demons either. I loved them because they listened to me. But just because I had friends who had more freedom than I did, did not mean that I would make poor choices. I overheard my mom say that I didn't get my menstrual cycle as often as my sister, and with the friends that I was hanging with, she feared the possibility that I could be pregnant. I turned on my portable CD player and listened to music until I had no more tears to shed and eventually fell asleep.

What remained consistent were the side-eyes from my mother and the ongoing suspicions that I might potentially be pregnant.

In June 2001 I was in 9th grade and attended the summer bridge program at Jane Addams Vocational High School. As I adjusted to my new school, what anyone thought of me seemed to matter less. This was especially true of my mother, who gave birth to fraternal twins in August 2001.

I went from watching only two siblings to a whopping four! If there was a reason to not get pregnant, I was truly living it. As the oldest of five children, the expectation was that I set the example for my younger siblings. Being in high school was a huge mile-stone for me as it meant that I only had *four* more years until my eighteenth birthday, and I could finally go away to college and live happily ever after!

Until then, I had to choose my vocation and I debated between cosmetology and nursing. Either one felt like a good choice because they were both sciences based. I learned how to braid when I was eight or nine years old, and the thought of getting paid on a professional level for that skill was exciting. Since I was a caregiver in some ways by nature, I also enjoyed some parts of helping people heal.

Around this time, I had a doctor's appointment at the teen clinic, the Urban Health El Nuevo San Juan, for my yearly physical before the official start of the school year. My mom was still recovering from childbirth, so I went to the clinic alone.

Dr. Gina was my new doctor. She was stylish, and always wore cute high-heeled shoes and she seemed genuinely interested when she would ask about how I was doing. During my appointment, she reviewed my chart and asked when my last menstrual cycle was. I couldn't remember. She began to talk about my irregular periods and mentioned PCOS (Polycystic Ovarian Syndrome). I had never heard of it.

Dr. Gina explained that PCOS is a hormonal disorder common among women of reproductive age who experience infrequent or prolonged menstrual periods and excess male hormone levels. The ovaries may develop numerous small collections of fluid (cysts) and fail to regularly release eggs.

FINALLY! I had an explanation for all of those missed monthly cycles. Not only was I telling the truth, but I also had science to back me up! No pregnancy, and no menopause.

Dr. Gina printed handouts on PCOS for me to review on my own. After the appointment, I went home excited to show my mom the good news! I opened our apartment door and my maternal grandmother was feeding my baby sister and signaled me to stay quiet as my mother was sleeping and holding my baby brother. I tip-toed upstairs and connected my computer to the phone jack so I could browse the internet on PCOS.

What I was reading was fascinating! There were some things I researched that didn't apply to me, like being overweight, or having high blood pressure. I didn't have those concerns, but my voice was a little deep for a girl. Maybe those androgen levels had something to do with being mistaken for my father every time I would answer the house phone!

Depression was also listed as a symptom. I didn't know what that meant, so I looked it up in the dictionary. This is my earliest memory of self-diagnosing depression. I felt sad a lot as a child, and in my adolescence, my anger was firmly rooted in feeling defeated. I was exhausted having to explain myself to my mother, only to be dismissed. Often I questioned why anyone would have children and teach them values, then not believe their children when they shared the truth. When I told my mother I wasn't doing anything with boys, it stung me terribly when she didn't believe me. It would take years for me to fully process and heal that hurt.

There were things I loved about my mother like her modest beginnings, she is the fourth child out of ten. My mom speaks Garifuna, Spanish and English, she moved to a country on her own to start a new life with the idea that her children will have opportunities that were not accessible to her.

I put a lot of my effort into reading and learning what I could do to minimize PCOS symptoms. Lifestyle changes were a consistent recommendation, so I started to make healthy changes. For most of high school, I was conscious about my diet. I started reading food labels and minimizing my sugar intake. If there was a word on a label that I could not pronounce, I decided that meant I shouldn't be eating it. As you can imagine, this completely limited what I could eat, considering my limited access to healthy foods at the time.

But I did everything I could to become healthier. I cut back on Kool-Aid, sodas, and juices, and I started drinking more water. I questioned food labels that said made with real meat, and in my mind I would think what was it made with before? I was more intentional about eating leafy greens and fruits. A few times out of the year I would completely stop eating meat and would notice a significant change in how I felt physically. Most significantly, my menstrual cycle would make its debut more frequently throughout the year than it ever had.

In January 2017 I decided to commit to a pescatarian diet, even though at times I would dabble as a vegetarian and vegan... I remember I ate a Texas Bacon Patty Melt at the Waffle House on New Year's Day of that year, and though I enjoyed it, it was the last time I would eat red meat. As I became more conscious of my choices and needs, I knew that shifting my diet would be better for my body, and I made the decision to be fully committed to consuming and using natural products.

I shared with my family new information as I learned it, but my mom was typically on the fence about my questioning established health practices I don't think I ever convinced her, but at very least she was listening to what I had to share.

As I became an adult, I learned healthy ways to cope with depression and PCOS. I learned to find wisdom in the wound and appreciate that although I had a right to be upset at what I experienced, my mother did the best she could.

To truly live a healthy holistic life with love it is imperative to use discernment and lead with the assumption that the people who love you lead with pure intent. I know now what my mother believed to be true was based on her limited experience and what she was taught about female body functions during reproductive age. Information that was true at one point can completely shift with access to knowledge that offers a broader lens.

One of the truths about healing is you have to be triggered in order to spark a reaction, then pause and consider. Only then, with clarity, choose to respond in a way that is in alignment with who you are in the present and not the past.

For a long time, I viewed my mother as a trigger. Her tone of voice, her choice of words, her nonchalance or dismissal of new information that didn't apply directly to her life, all had a direct effect on my feelings. I had to choose to be curious, I had to choose to be compassionate, I had to choose to be caring and gentle with the notion that in the way I have evolved from adolescence to adulthood, my mother had also evolved in her journey of motherhood.

When my perception transcended I was able to actively forgive and gradually validate, then release my anger, and let that part of me step back and let the other parts of me step up.

There were six (6) key factors – actions of forgiveness – that allowed me to genuinely let go and restructure how I interact with my mama:

**Forgiveness Factor #1:** Validate your feelings of anger. I was not mad for no reason. Pretending that it's taboo to feel is detrimental to progress. It is okay to feel anger, process the 'feels' and be curious about the root of the issue. Seek behavioral health services as needed.

**Forgiveness Factor #2:** Find the wisdom in the wound. When I put my feelings aside (briefly) and processed what I learned from the experience, I recognized that my body needed me to be intentional about the management of my health. Be mindful of your growth. What do you do better as a result?

**Forgiveness Factor #3:** Assume the best. This part is more for yourself than the other person. My mother was not incorrect in her logic, but her thinking was dated. As a result, it was challenging for her to comprehend something new. I believe that my mother always loved me and everything that she did, or was unable to do, was her best at the moment.

**Forgiveness Factor #4:** Shift the narrative. This part is difficult, because when you are triggered you can be flooded with memories of the past and your body will remember how you felt in the past. Pause, take a DEEP breath and allow the feeling to pass. Focus on the present and be intentional about responding in the present

**Forgiveness Factor #5:** Practice, practice, and practice! Every single day brainstorm ways to be intentional about fostering a healthy relationship with your mom. Create new traditions.

**Forgiveness Factor #6:** Grow together. I learned to be intentional about including my mother in my life decisions and consulting her for help when I needed it. When you need help, reach out to her; you just may be surprised by what your mama can support you through.

My relationship with my mother has shifted over the years and we are in a better space. Going away to college didn't solve my life problems, and I didn't find a 'happily ever after' fairytale ending. Instead, the experience I actually lived helped me create a 'naturally ever after,' living holistically from a place of love, healing, and gratitude.

# Therapy Now in Session:
# How Having a Breakdown Built Me Up and Banished the Monster Within

*By Michele Mikki Jones*

*"The world will change when women reclaim their power as the sane, nurturing hands of love, which are ever reaching to cultivate a world of beauty, safety and harmony."*

*– Bryant McGill*

Have you ever been called out on an issue that you thought you had so carefully hidden from not only the world, but from yourself as well? You thought you had buried it so deep that no amount of digging could ever unearth it!

That's what I had done with the pain of being my mother's child. I had covered up so much hurt and sorrow that I had become numb to love. The heaviness of the burden of living a life feeling unloved, unwanted and unneeded by the one person I cherished the most was just unbearable and I suppressed it.

What follows here is an account of how the masked emotions of a broken child stifled me as an adult, restricting me from the feelings of love and acceptance, kindness, and affection to the point where the brokenness almost killed what I was fighting so hard to give life to: my family! This is my story of how forgiving my mother saved my life and set me on a healing path to saving my daughters.

## THE DENIAL:

You have got to be freakin' kidding me!!! You want me to do WHAT?!!! *You heard me. I want you to call your mother, apologize and offer forgiveness.*

I know I heard you, but are you serious?! *Isn't that why you are here? To begin taking a different approach towards life and how you live it?*

But apologizing to my mother is neither my goal nor my problem! *Isn't it?*

NO! My problem is the guilt of not seeing the pain in my children's eyes. My problem is understanding how I could have ignored their cries for help! *I understand that. But do you understand why you hadn't done all the things you just mentioned?*

That's what you are here for! *No. I am here to assist you in under-standing all that you want to know. At least psychologically.*

OK, Doc. So tell me this. How does apologizing to my mother and forgiving my mother get me to understanding why and how I can lift this guilt of "missing shit" with my children? *I thought one of your goals was to stop cussing?*

It is. But right now you are fucking with my head and I'm not focused on "NOT CUSSING"! You want me to do something that has NOT A DAMN thing to do with the problem I am having with my daughters! *Are you sure about that?*

Here we go again! Yeah! I am VERY SURE! (This lady right HERE! She is about to piss me ALL the way OFF!) Need I reiterate my goals to you?

**One:** get rid of the guilt.
**Two:** learn new ways to communicate effectively with my children.
**Three:** change the tone and the language in which I speak.
**Four:** create a loving and nurturing environment.

Those are my goals. You made me write them down and then repeat them until they stuck. You said that by doing this I wouldn't lose sight of why I am here. *That's right. I said that, and had you do exactly what you repeated. So now that I am requesting you do something else that will get you to your goals, why are you so resistant?*

AND BOOM! THERE IT IS! The question that propelled me into the depths of my unforgiving soul. The catalyst that caused me to break from all the lies that I had been telling myself. The infamous straw that broke the camel's back. And in this case, I am that camel (at least metaphorically speaking).

It is the summer of 2007 and things are just starting to settle down. We had just gone through one of the most difficult times of our lives, a time that lasted for four long grueling ass years.

The house is finally getting to be quiet. But the silence is killing me. Not because I don't respect the peace and quiet. NO! It is killing me because we – my children and I – are walking around like zombies. We are barely having conversations. We rarely have more than a cordial "hello" or "good morning" to say to one another. And unless we are talking about the babies (my two oldest grand-daughters), we don't have shit to say to one another.

It was a clear beautiful day. The sky was filled with puffed white clouds. The girls were outside playing in front of the house and all I can think as I look down at their happy little faces is – I have had enough! It was crazy the way the feeling just came over me! It was like a wind had blown and rocked me to the very core of my being. And in just that moment I knew that if I didn't find a way to fix this, this ill-fated situation of mis – non – communication, WE – MY FAMILY – would forever be broken. So, on this beautiful summer day, I decided that I was taking my ass back to therapy!

Therapy wasn't new to me. I had been a few times before. I thought about asking my children to go with me, but they had put up such a stink when I had them go when they were younger, that I didn't want to even mention it to them now. In hindsight, knowing what I know now, I should have kicked my own ass and just asked if they wanted to go.

The first time I went to therapy was after the rape. That lasted all of 3 months before I started to feel that I could deal with my trauma on my own as opposed to sitting with these people trading war stories of how to not blame ourselves. Hell – he raped me! My only fault was that I thought he was a friend. The rest – NOPE! ALL ON HIM!

The second time I found myself in therapy was just after receiving my diagnosis of lupus. I fell into a horrible pit of depression and was preparing myself to die. That little pity party ended in November 2005. I had two new opportunities to get this (grand) mothering shit right.

The third time I began therapy because the guilt was just too much to handle and with the weight of everything else going on in my life, I was about to suffocate.

I was feeling that as a mother I failed my children. I allowed evil to invade our home and enter our lives and cause us hurt beyond measure and pain beyond repair – or so I thought. Because I did not know how to acknowledge the "monster within", my children were forced to live without: without safety; without security; without confidence in myself. What I was giving them was a show. The intent was good, but the reality was just, well, unreal. I thought that if I showed them what a strong, hardworking woman looked like, if I showed them how a real woman handled her business, if I showed them that big girls don't cry, I would be able to continue to cover-up the fact that I was weak and broken, scared and lonely. I was hiding.

Like the stories that children tell of monsters under their beds, the fear of pulling back the edges of the covers and looking to see exactly what they are afraid of, I was hiding from the pain of rejection, the disappointment of love and the sorrow of being alone.

Again, in hindsight, I should have just let them see the hurt in me. I should have just let them see me.

Anyway, I was sitting in therapy and we were four sessions in, and the conversation shifts to my mother and me. Just a few questions about how I felt about her. What role she plays in my life. What was she like when I was growing up. Nothing too deep. Just trivial conversation. All part of therapy, right?

In the beginning sessions, I was allowed to release all of those hurt feelings of guilt and shame about the choices I had made in my relationships and in my marriage that had caused such turmoil in the lives of my children. I was FINALLY allowed to deal with the ugliness of the rape that had sent me into a downward spiral that I didn't even know I was spinning in. I was able to accept responsibility for not seeing what I should have seen regarding the abuse. I was able to acknowledge the truth about my impulsive behaviors, which lead to me making some not so very good choices.

I had to allow myself to admit that instead of confronting the abuse issue involving my daughters head-on, I chose revenge instead. I had to admit that my misguided idea that if he hurt me, I could hurt him back was all WRONG! Instead of making the situation better, I only hurt my children and myself more.

Those last two acknowledgments were DOOZIES! Because this was where the majority of my guilt lay.

Now we are coming towards the end of session four and my therapist tells me to prepare myself for progressive homework for the next session. I shrug my shoulders and say, "OK."

One week later and we are at the top of session five and this high priced professional psychologist is telling me that my assignment for this session is to call my mother—who I haven't spoken to IN YEARS—apologize to her, and offer her my forgiveness.

## THE RESISTANCE

WHHHOOOOOAAAAA! Wait just one good gosh damn minute!

If you don't take your even-toned speaking ass outta here, I'm gonna cuss you like you have never heard! Why in the WORLD would I even want to speak to her! And why are we even talking about HER! She is not even a relevant factor in my life! What does my relationship with my children have to do with HER! She doesn't even want them to call her grandma!

Are you fucking serious?! She left me! She abandoned me! She gave me away! She ignored me! She HURT ME! Why in THE HELL would you even suggest that I even call her... let alone APOLOGIZE!

Are you legal?!?! What school did you attend?! I need a whole new therapist! (If this is what the beginning of having a full and total breakdown feels like – then it's on!)

And for almost 15 minutes she just let me rant like a lunatic, never changing her tone, never flinching at my verbal assault, never answering a question without a question, or making a statement that didn't bring the ownership of the situation right back to me.

Then she hit me with: "Why are you so resistant?"

Pure silence! Mouth wide open. Eyes bulging. I was left utterly speechless. It was like the question had captured my tongue and attacked my senses. And as the words weaved their way through the recesses of my mind all I could think was, if she, my mother, did ALL these horrible, uncaring, neglectful things to me and I had literally done nothing to her, except be born, shouldn't she be apologizing to me? What good does it do me to apologize to her?

For so long, we, as a people, have been taught that you only need to apologize for what you do wrong. That's not always true. There are times when you need to apologize for the way you allow people to treat you, thereby setting them on notice that you will no longer be accepting such behavior and that you FORGIVE them. You are not apologizing for their behavior, you are apologizing for your response to their behavior.

Just as you are not forgiving them for them, you are forgiving them for you!

Because I held resentment towards my mother for the things she had done (or not done) I never really opened my heart up to receive love and affection. I was always guarded and unsure. I questioned everyone's motive for even speaking to me. I just knew that if you talked to me you wanted something from me. And on those rare occasions when I did let someone in, it wasn't for long. I would find a way to have to leave before they asked me to stay. Staying was not something that I did well.

Over time I had taught myself to be comfortable with restless-ness. I created my own state of ADD (Attention Deficient Disorder) for myself. My grandmothers tried to help me when I was younger by having me live with them, but the laws were different and grand-parents didn't really have rights in the '70s. So my stays with them were always cut short by screaming matches in the neighborhood streets, followed by police cars, which lead to clinical evaluations and eventually court orders.

As for my father, I was afraid of him. My mother had told me on so many occasions that he wasn't my father, I couldn't bring myself to love him for fear that he would leave me, too. I was a defenseless pawn in a parental game of chess that I didn't even know I was playing.

And so, there I was, this forty-year-old woman, sitting in this beautiful book-lined office with solid oak furniture, handcrafted with details as intricate as fine porcelain, made in places I have yet to learn the names of, crying and screaming at the top of my lungs at a woman who didn't even flinch at anything I was saying.

At that moment, I felt like a child who has just had her favorite doll's head ripped right from her shoulders. I felt like a little girl who has just lost her best friend.

To say I was devastated would be an understatement. At age forty, wife, mother, mid-level salaried executive, and homeowner, I was acting like a scared, broken child. My epiphany was finally arriving! My breakthrough was almost here!

In that one defining moment, with that one simple question—*why are you so resistant?*—with that one massive outburst, I finally started to understand why I had missed it with my children.

Because I had never seen it in myself. BREATHE!

## THE ACCEPTANCE

After I regained my voice and was able to gather my thoughts, the room had calmed down (mainly me) and the chairs had been righted (not that they had been overturned), I simply said:

I am not paying you for this!

*OK*


(God, I wanted to punch her smug ass right in the face! But instead I picked up the phone and I took another deep breath – WWWWOOOOOOO!)


Picking up that phone and making that call was one of the hardest things I had ever had to do. And that babysitting professional therapist standing directly over my shoulder, looking at every number I pushed wasn't helping!

Dialing those ten digits, I was praying that no one would answer. But she did, and when I heard her voice, I broke. The tears were everywhere. It took me a good ten or twenty seconds to even get a voice clear enough to say hello. It took another few seconds or so to then inquire as to her well-being. And for the next ten minutes, my mother told me of all that I had missed in her life over the past twelve years, and I listened. Never once interrupting. Only answering with the simplest YES or NO. I just listened.

## THE FORGIVENESS

Nearing the end of this seemingly one-sided conversation – I had told her nothing of my life, nothing of the lives of my children, nothing about us at all – I finally said, "Mommy, I apologize for not being the daughter you expected me to be, and I forgive you for treating me as such."

OOOH, MY FUCKING GOODNESS! THERE IT IS!
MY BREAKTHROUGH!

Where did these words come from? Whose voice was this speaking? I began crying all over again. Not because of how she responded, but because I realized that I no longer cared! I no longer cared that she didn't listen to me when I told her what her boyfriends did to me when I was younger. I no longer cared that she beat me mercilessly with extension cords and heeled shoes for sins that I had no part in. I no longer cared that she willingly and whole-heartedly gave me away, oftentimes to family, sometimes even to strangers. All I cared about was what I had done, and was doing, to MY CHILDREN because of what she had done to me!

She hurt me!

With those three words – I FORGIVE YOU – I found freedom.
With those three words – I FORGIVE YOU – I found clarity.
With those three words – I FORGIVE YOU – I found peace.

To this day, I can't even tell you what her response to my words was. I truly don't remember. Actually, I don't even think I heard her. My eyes were so swollen and wet with tears, my ears overflowing with years of words being spoken from the silence of my thoughts, and my heart so full of a different kind of emotion that I had yet to describe, know and understand, I don't even remember hanging up the phone.

What I do remember is that after the call, my therapist and I examined some pretty revealing behaviors. The first behavior we talked about is not what you think – that I cried when she answered. NOPE. That was the second.

The first behavior that we acknowledged was the fact that after all the years of not speaking to my mother, I had never deleted her number from my phone, nor had I erased it from my memory. I picked up the phone like it was habit and punched in the numbers like I was dialing my own home. TALK ABOUT REVELATION!

The third thing that we talked about concerned my current feelings about how my relationship with my mother affected my relationship with my children. I cried yet again. Call me a Weeping Willow, but these tears were different.

You can perceive the phone call anyway that you like and refer to it how you will, but for me, this is the session where I truly began ridding myself of the monster inside me. I was finally ready to pull back the edge of the covers of my hidden soul and face my demons head-on.

No more would I be that soul buried alive deep in the earth crying and clawing for release. No more would I withdraw into myself to become lost in the misery that once was my past. No more would I allow harm to come to my children or grandchildren because I chose to suffer through unforgiveness and shame. No more would I abandon my heart.

No, this day was a new growing day. A day of learning new ways of thinking, learning new ways of being, learning new ways of living. Today is the day the monster is no more.

As adults, as grown men and women, we want so faithfully to believe that our relationships with our children have no correlation with the relationships we had or have with our mothers. Quite the contrary. We learn our life's patterns of conduct and behavior from those who raised us. Whether biological or adoptive, our rearing environment, the culture in which we are brought up, affects and influences our growth.

There are elements of our existence that are inherited, but the majority of our behaviors, actions, and attitudes, we pick up as we grow up. If you grow up in a family that doesn't sit down to dinner as a unit and have "how'd your day go" type conversations, as an adult, it is not a practice that you hold with high regard in others. If you grow up in a family that doesn't believe in open expressions of affection, as an adult you lack the skill of cultivating empathetic relationships. These types of learned or unlearned behaviors are what we unwittingly pass on to our children.

Subconsciously we understand these behaviors to be a way of life, when in actuality, they are not. They are a sign of dysfunction. Our families have held on to so much hurt, envy, guilt, shame, disappointment, and anger for so long, we have convinced ourselves it is the norm.

It's NOT!!!

Dysfunctionally functional – the idea that if I keep my mouth shut and my eyes closed all that I think is bad will be a dream and everything will be normal again – is an overblown, unrealistic concept that needs to be permanently erased from the minds of us all. It stems from the old adage of "what goes on in this house stays in this house".

Consciously, we need to STOP THE BULLSHIT, OPEN THE DAMN DOOR AND WALK THE FUCK OUT! There is not a thing normal about the sins that go on behind closed doors.

We need to know that our mother/daughter relationships are pivotal to a rightly functioning society. Why? Because not only do we teach our daughters, but we also teach our sons. Much of the chaos in our families is rooted in the mental agility of our mothers. If their mind isn't right, neither is the family dynamic. Now, you may say "who gets to define what a rightly functioning society is"? WELL – YOU DO!!!

We are all born with a nature of trust and until someone violates that trust, we continue to believe in it. But once that trust is violated, the lies begin, the misdeeds take place, the stealing happens and what has always felt so right now feels so horribly wrong. This violation of trust leaves us with mothers burying their sons and daughters not understanding the priceless value of the essence of their worth. Once trust is broken, it is one of the hardest confidences to regain.

But it can be done.

## THE HEALING

To say my relationship with my mother got a whole lot better after that call in my therapist's office would be a lie. For while that call snatched the scab off some very old wounds, many of which had festered and had become poison in my soul. Emotions that I had buried deep within or ones that I simply refused to acknowledge had to come forth in order for me even to begin the healing process. And make no mistake about it, healing is a process.

The issues that I had to deal with between my mother and me

were massive. It would take several more years to clean out all the nasty, disgusting feelings. Anger and resentment, hurt and pain, most of which I hadn't realized I harbored, lived not only in my soul but in my heart and mind as well. I undeniably had to learn to be affectionate. I unequivocally had to learn to be vulnerable. I had to become unafraid. And if I thought the phone call was bad, the healing process (at least the beginning) was worse.

I cannot say for anyone else what that process is like, but for me, the process involved taking specific steps:

- First, I had to learn to be real with myself about who I am and how I feel. This first step helped me regain my life.
- Second, I had to accept others for who and where they are in life. This step allowed me to be more open-minded and less judgmental.
- Third, I had to learn not to take the blame for the actions of others. Yet another step that helped me to know I was ready to forgive.

It's like navigating the stages of grief. We all do it differently but hopefully come to the same result: ACCEPTANCE!

Please understand, I am not telling you that you need to get a grip and take your tail to therapy and work shit out. No. I am telling you that therapy worked for me, HOW it worked for me and WHY I would recommend it for you. The presence of an unbiased non-judgmental opinion is a weight lifter.

If you do choose therapy, you can go in there with all your ready lies if you want to, but a trained professional, a knowledgeable professional, will be able to see right through them and tell you that you are wasting your money and their time.

But not if you are REALLY READY! If you are really wanting to mend the break, bridge the gap, and/or fill the void of being a daughter living a life without her mother – SEEK help and be ready to PUT IN THE WORK!

I went to therapy to work on my relationship with my children. Remember, we had been through some serious shit and I was bearing the heaviest load of guilt I could carry. My shoulders were getting tired and the pain was causing a depressing anguish that I no longer felt I could handle.

I finished therapy understanding my relationship with my mother, and why that relationship dictated the course of all my other relationships.

Suffice it to say that after years of consistent and continual effort, I now speak to my mother at least once every week or so. I keep myself informed of her well-being by having her doctor's appointments booked through me, and I tell her 'I love you' at the beginning and end of every call – and I mean it.

No, she hasn't said 'I'm sorry' or 'I accept your apology,' and no, I am not expecting it. Now that I am healing I no longer need to hear it. In fact, if she did say either of those things, I am not sure she would fully understand what she is sorry or apologizing for.

What she does say is, "baby I'm so proud of you," and that is music to my ears. Not because I need her affirmation of my success, but simply because I know she means it.

## THE LESSON LEARNED

So, when you get to a point where you feel that there is nothing left to salvage of the relationship between you and your mother, here are a few realizations that I learned from the missed relationship with my mother that will hopefully encourage you to give her the benefit of YOUR doubt and try again:

- **Blame is transferable** – don't bullshit yourself into believing that it is all her fault. It's not. No, you didn't ask to be here but you are and maybe, just maybe you didn't come with a How-to-Guide and she had to learn as she went along.
- **Age is more than a number** – regardless of whether she is a teen mom or a middle-aged executive, if her mental capacity is not fully functional, her emotional response is damn near non-existent. Just because she is older, it doesn't make her better at mothering if her mindset isn't right.
- **It sucks being the oldest or the only** – being the oldest of however many of you there are or the only of one, means that you were the "tester". You were the prototype. Don't get so caught up and angry about how she treats the others. She just didn't know better.
- **She was once a child** – before you start dogging her out for all the mistakes she made with raising or not raising you, understand her background. Once you can see where and what she comes from, then you can find out where you are going.

- **Remorse is real** – never underestimate the power of forgiveness and never give in to the powerlessness of being afraid. Learn to use your voice – even if it sounds like your mother's.

-  **Judgment is a lonely place** – until you've walked a mile in her shoes, don't you dare question the height of her heels. Whether she clicks high in heels, tips softly in slippers, or pounds pavement in sneakers, her journey is just that, her journey, and she is navigating it at her acceptable pace.

- **Trust can and WILL be reborn** – were her lies intentional? Was the pain planned? Are the feelings mutual? Stop trying to rebuild on what you know to be broken. Start building on what is sure. We can't go back to fix our mistakes, but we surely don't have to pay for them with the rest of our lives.

- **Call it a lesson learned** – according to you, she didn't get it right, but it is not your job to show her how it's done. NO! Your job is to respect the teacher and perfect the lesson. Parenting is a hypothesis that changes with every theory. It doesn't necessarily mean that the old hypothesis is wrong, it just means that the expected result has changed.

- **Don't forget to take out the trash** – All words are not gospel and recollections are not pure. Learn for yourself what is real in any given situation. Take what you need from it and leave the rest for someone else.

- **Mind your manners** – If not her, someone taught you respect – exercise that learning at ALL TIMES!

I pray nothing but peace and tranquility be with you as you embrace forgiveness and speak life into that which you once thought had been buried forever. Unearth your true self, know that there will be pain, but continue on and I guarantee you, your healing will come.

We've all made decisions based on good intentions that didn't turn out the way we expected. We've all said some things with the hopes of encouraging others only to have them hear it with offence. We've all experienced a hurt that we felt was beyond forgiveness, but somehow we learned to move on. Life shapes us and molds us based on our individual experiences and responses. It's not about who you were; it's about how you factor that learning into who you've become. Only apologize for that which you fail to do, knowing that you only fail to do that which you do not seek to achieve.

What are you allowing life to make of you?

# Loyal to Dysfunction

*By Mrs. Cynthia Williams-Bey*

*A loyal woman is admirable until she realizes her King
has a queen that he's already given his last name.*

The first time I saw him, I was walking from my Brooklyn office cubicle heading towards the cafeteria to grab some lunch. He was tall, muscular, hazel-eyed, and walking towards me. Of course, I acted like I didn't notice him. But by the next week, we had exchanged numbers. We began to talk, and then we started to hang out after work. We were friends just kicking it at first, but then it quickly turned into something else. I was feeling him, he was feeling me and we started staying at each other's cribs. We spent so much time together, and it felt like there was nothing we couldn't say or do around each other. We were smoking, drinking and sexing every chance we got.

I also learned pretty quickly he had a baby on the way by a chick in Virginia, but according to him, they had no intentions to get married or to be together, so I rolled with it. Eventually, I was introduced to his family and began spending time with them, so I was falling even harder for him. Like falling in love.

On a Monday morning after a long weekend, we got to work and learned the company we worked for was bankrupt and going out of business. To make matters worse, I got home and learned that the place I was staying was being sold.

With no family to turn to, I worried about what I would do with no job and no home. My last encounter with my family resulted in my grandmother's house being torn up, as me, my sister, and nieces fought one another like we were strangers.

The last time I saw my dad was after my mother's death when he called me a little bitch and then took the last of my mother's belongings and moved them to his other children's mother's house up the road.

I've never had an issue getting a job, but for some reason, I couldn't seem to get an interview or whenever I went on an interview I wouldn't get hired. On the other end, he's making plans to move to Virginia to be closer to his expected child. After some convincing, he finally got me to put some applications in for jobs in Virginia and take a road trip with him to have some interviews.

Things unfolded as if they were meant to be. We went to see a spot on the southside of Richmond, and it was affordable so we took it. I went on my second interview and they offered me the position right on the spot. I was excited and feeling great. As we were heading back to Brooklyn after our trip, I got a call from the apartment complex stating that we were approved.

Moving day arrived, and we were due to move in and start our new jobs, our new lives, all in the same day. I left Brooklyn and never looked back.

Now we were fully in this 'situationship,' working and living together. He had a baby on the way, so of course, he visited his baby's mother. As time went on, I was left in the house alone for hours and he was coming home at all times of the night. For me, this wasn't a big deal because this was how it was for me growing up. My dad was never home. Though he lived with us, I only saw him on occasion. He was always working and saving lives. So I was in this relationship and what should have been a red flag to me was overlooked because, hey, this was what I was used to. I was going to trust him and hold him down just like my mom did for my dad. Why should I have thought differently? Man, was I so wrong.

Months went by. Not only did we work together but we had a car and a whole apartment together. Love became stupidity. There was always a new girl in the picture, followed up with one of his famous apologies.

After some time, we decided to share the apartment together but no longer be together officially. Following a trip from Brooklyn, I came home and he said he was heading out to pick up a friend. Little did I know that this was a female friend that he had relations with. I could tell he didn't tell her who I was based on her interaction with me. I went into my room and left them to talk, then I heard the bedroom door close. I was in my room in disbelief because I couldn't believe he had the audacity to bring this chick to our crib and we ain't even been separated for a hot 48 hours!

As I sat in the opposite bedroom the tears streamed down and all I could think was how could the man that I loved do this to me? I could hear the chemistry of their bodies and as every second went by the sound and intensity of their lust grew louder. I could no longer bear the pain.

This is ENOUGH, I thought as I jumped out of my bed and lunged towards his bedroom door and began banging on it. Feeling rage and betrayal, I demanded that she be taken out of my home. She gathered her things and they proceeded out the door.

As time passed, I was still in complete disbelief and shock that I, a girl so full of life, passion, intelligence, and values, would succumb to these circumstances. How did I allow myself to be in such a dysfunctional relationship? When did I send him the message that it was acceptable to treat me this way?

Not only did I take up with a man who had a child on the way, but I also moved and rearranged my whole entire life to be with him. No proposal, no marriage, but I packed up my life and moved to an entirely different state with no family or support at all. And now he was bringing other women into my home.

I began to ask myself some important and difficult questions. I began to ask why I was willing to compromise my worth. I questioned why I ignored so many red flags. I wondered where I learned to tolerate being treated so badly.

The reality was that I was a product of my environment and my upbringing. I was a child in an adult body trying to be a loyal woman just as my mom was to my dad. My childhood environment played a major part in my decisions as an adult. It was like the environment I was once in caused me to become a victim unknowingly. But it wouldn't be long before I would realize just how much of my environment I had become.

My dad was the neighborhood hero that was responsible for saving the lives of the people in our community. This was at a time when the actual Emergency Response workers were scared to respond to the calls in our neighborhood due to fear of being the next victim. Perhaps it was that hero syndrome that attracted a young high school drop out who was already a single mother of four children. Perhaps it was his ability to gather people together as the neighborhood DJ, Godfather Rock. It may even have been his strength and courage as a Military Police Officer.

As a child, I remember how beautiful my mom was. She took care of most of the children in the neighborhood and she cared for my siblings and me the best way she could. I also watched how my mom catered to my Father in my young years. How she ironed his clothes, made sure he had a hot cooked meal and warm bath when he came off of his shift at night.

I also saw how many nights my mom stayed alone. I saw how my dad came and went as he pleased. I saw the different women hanging around his business pretending to be a worker or student at his establishment. I saw how close my half-siblings and I were in age. I saw that my mom was ok with all of it. My mom never argued with him or any of the other women. I never saw her talk down to my father. I never heard her say he was no good. She always referred to him as a good man.

But there were so many times I would sit staring at the door waiting for his return.

Sometimes it would be days and sometimes it would be months, but this somehow came to seem normal. This is what I believed happened in every family. Never did I see my mother with or around any other man. She waited and anticipated his return, just as I was doing now.

Now I was sitting in my mother's same position, being a good woman to the wrong man. But my situation was so much worse. I went from loving the wrong man to almost dying by the hands of that wrong man.

After a weekend away, I returned to our apartment, and he began to question me about my whereabouts during my trip. He became more and more furious at the thought of me possibly being with another man. I backed away into my room hoping to escape. He rushed me and slammed my back against a mirror on the wall. Pieces of the mirror shattered all over me and fell to the floor, as memories of my mother shattered in my mind.

I fell on the bed and felt the sharpness of the knife he held to my throat. My life flashed before my eyes and I drifted back to that moment as a child when I walked in to see my sister's blood splattered across the closet door from being beaten by her husband. I drifted more and I saw myself as a child in the hallway of the projects, scared and frightened as I saw the blood smeared across the building hallway from my sister being beaten by her child's father.

As my life continued to flash before my eyes, I could see the darkness and rage in his pupils. I mustered enough strength to call on the name of Jesus. Although I didn't know Him personally, I had heard how He saved so many from deathly encounters. As I began to call out for His help, my lover began to release me. At that very moment, a loud banging began at the door. I quickly got up and ran to my Divine help, and as I opened the door a familiar face was upon me. I was in such fear that I ran to the corner and balled up in a fetal position. I was consoled and quickly taken out of the apartment.

It would be nice if I could tell you that this incident was my wake-up call, but the reality was this was just the first of several dysfunctional relationships I endured as a result of something much deeper and generational. As I began to dig deeper, I found a lost little girl still hurting and traumatized by her childhood – a childhood that included, poverty, domestic violence, and adultery.

I grew to become a woman plagued with memories of playing in the neighborhood with all her friends, but enduring the conversations and whispers about the mother she loved and looked up to. I was a child who routinely overheard the whispers of her mother being with a man who was not only married to someone else, but who had 10+ kids and several other women not including his wife. Imagine being called a bastard and having a grown woman hate you for being living evidence of her husband's infidelity.

The injury all that whispering causes hurts like hell. It's a feeling that never leaves, a feeling that causes you to battle depression. It's a feeling that causes you to be promiscuous because you are trying to fill the void from the love you never received as a child. A feeling that will cause you to cluster unforgiveness and bitterness in your heart. It's a feeling that will cause you to feel a sense of betrayal from the one woman that you admired, and thought could do no wrong; that woman for me was my mom.

As women, we often fail to realize how our actions can have a lasting effect on our children. My mother was the best provider she could be, and she did the best she could under the circumstances. My mother didn't neglect me, and she didn't treat me badly. She showed me how to cook and clean and how to carry myself as a young lady. Without her knowing it, she also taught me some other things, like how to be faithful and cater to your man. The only problem was I learned how to be faithful to a man who didn't honor me, and for whom I was not a priority, for whom I was on reserve, and who belonged to many others.

If anything, I learned how to be loyal to dysfunction. As I reflect on my relationships, I realize most of the men I was involved with resembled my dad—the same characteristics, the same demeanor, the same tribe of children with different women.

I didn't just wake up one day and decide to be with a man who wasn't fully mine, but a true rolling stone. What I experienced was a learned behavior. We may have choices, but that doesn't negate the power upbringing and surroundings play in our adult lives.

According to the article, *Factors That Affect Growth and Development in Children,* three of the top ten factors that influence the growth and development of a child are environment, family influence, and learning and reinforcement.[1] I'm evidence of that as are so many other women. You think a side chick learned how to be that way on her own? You think a woman with standards and high self-esteem learned that on her own? Not at all. Someone or something from her childhood influenced who she is now. It could have influenced her in a good way or a bad way. Most of our characteristics, beliefs, and behaviors are often rooted in either the presence or absence of our mothers.

I became an adult caught in this cycle of dysfunctional romances with men that wouldn't commit, trying to figure out what was wrong with me, and desperately seeking the love I deserved.

---

1 https://parenting.firstcry.com

One day, as I was talking to my son's father on the phone, I remember saying to him, "I don't care what you do just as long as it doesn't come to our home." It was in that moment I had a flashback to my childhood and all I could think was I was becoming my mother.

As I continued to reflect I remember feeling so angry and disappointed at my mom for allowing someone to treat her that way, and for not showing me a better way. She never warned me to stay away from guys like this. Instead, her example made me think it was appropriate to be loyal to a man who was not faithful. She allowed me to grow up in an environment where I witnessed my sisters being betrayed and beaten by their husbands, just for them to make up and remain in the house like nothing happened. I was angry and hurt and I didn't understand where to direct my feelings.

I eventually came to the realization that I was angry, and had unsettled feelings towards my mom. The most challenging part for me was dealing with all those feelings since she had passed on and was gone. Forgiving my mom wasn't the hardest part; admitting that I was feeling this way and not being able to express it to her was the most heartbreaking. I felt like I was betraying her and dishonoring her in her death by being angry at her. I had to realize that my journey wasn't really about her but it was about me. First, I had to admit my anger and deal with those feelings so I was able to acknowledge the areas in my life that needed a change. Second, I had to identify everything inside me that was wounded so I could begin to heal. Third, I had to forgive not only my mom but I had to first forgive myself.

My mother was a beautiful and loving woman who tried to be

a good mother and partner. I can never sit with her and say why she did what she did or how she felt. What I can say is I trust that she did what she thought was best for my siblings and me.

Perhaps she stuck with one man because she was protecting us from something. Perhaps she didn't want to expose my siblings and me to the possibility of a man who wasn't our father molesting or hurting us because we weren't his children.

Even though my mother made mistakes, I had to understand that her mistakes didn't have to continue with me. I had a choice to either continue my cycle of dysfunction and abusive relationships leaning on the excuse that I was a product of my environment, or I could use what I learned about my life and my legacy to strive for better.

Just as my mom had a choice, I have one, too. And so do you. In order for change to occur in any situation, someone must be willing to point out the problem and change it. You can't bring forth real change with an unforgiving heart. As Marianne Williamson wrote, "unforgiveness is like drinking poison and waiting for the other person to die."

I have forgiven my mother. I forgave her and in forgiving her I was finally able to identify the generational cycle of dysfunction that has plagued my bloodline. And I am finally able to overcome it.

Now I'm able to do better with my children. I'm able to show them that real love starts with loving myself, and loving them enough to model healthy behavior and empowering choices.

I don't know what you may have endured or what has caused you to hold blame in your heart, but it's time for you to put the poison down and live. This isn't about your mother, but about you.

It's about you finally being free to live and have a fulfilling life from a place of wholeness and not a place of brokenness.

Love isn't defined by how someone makes you feel but by how you make yourself feel. Regardless of your background or experience, you don't have to settle for someone mistreating you. You are beautiful and you are worthy of love and you deserve loyalty without dysfunction.

# Coming Full Circle:
# My Forgiveness Journey
### By Winifred A. Winston

*"I can be changed by what happens to me,*
*but I refuse to be reduced by it."*

*– Maya Angleou*

**"**STOP! Just Stop! Let her go!"

I stood in the walkway of the ICU where only seconds before I had watched hospital staff slide a wooden board under my mother. I stood stiff with tears streaming down my face as a nurse climbed on top of her doing chest compressions. I watched as they shot medicine into her IV. Her blood pressure would rise and immediately fall again. They repeated this a few times before I screamed at the top of my lungs. STOP! Just stop! Let her go! I heard a long beep, and within minutes, I felt my mother leave her body. My older sister stood crying beside me and later told me she felt something in that moment, too. Later, our older brother would share that around the time she left us, he awoke sleepwalking trying to turn on lights. I was only 25 and my mother was gone.

I often say I lost her twice, first to a stroke when I was 23. The stroke left her unable to speak, eat or walk. She was bedridden. Then at 25, she succumbed to the cocktail of chemotherapy I reluctantly approved after surgery to remove a large mass of colon cancer.

The truth is, I had lost and rediscovered my mother many, many times over the course of my childhood.

Hazel Mae Finkley was the mother of four children. Kenny and Sonya, her eldest, were from an early relationship when she was in her 20's. In her 30's, she met and married my father, Fred Douglas Winston, who already had four children from his first marriage. Together he and my mother had two children: first Johnathan, and three years later, me. Together we were a blended family of eight children.

My parents divorced when I was only two years old, so I have no recollection of my biological father ever being part of my life. As he planned to leave my mother, he told her he was establishing things in North Carolina and we'd all relocate to North Carolina as a family. Instead, he took up with another woman, with whom he had a child only one year younger than me. When Fred left my mother, he sent me to live with his mother Remel in Harlem, New York when I was only two years old, and he took my five-year-old brother, Johnathan, to raise down south in North Carolina.

I was five years old when my single mother came for me and took me to live with her in Brooklyn, New York with my two other siblings, Kenny and Sonya. My father and Johnathan never really visited much, and it would be years before I actually saw my brother again. I remember seeing pictures of him and I knew I had a brother who was tall, slim and the only sibling that shared the same mother and father as me, but I longed for the day to meet him. I just knew he'd be my best friend, and the big brother I never had.

Life in Brooklyn quickly started to shape itself. My mother, now a single mom of three, was a Licensed Practical Nurse (LPN), who worked in long term care and consistently kept two full-time jobs. We lived in a brownstone on Lincoln Place, which she purchased in the 1960s with her younger brother, who died of a massive heart attack before I was born. She often rented out rooms, so we always had a house full of tenants. Kenny and Sonya attended a private school for most of elementary and middle school. My mother also met and started dating a Jamaican man named Joe Plumber.

Sadly, things started to take a drastic turn in our house. My brother, Kenny, twelve years older than me, dropped out of high school and began drinking a lot. He became physically abusive, and I don't recall him ever holding down a job. Later, my sister, Sonya, six years older than me, became a teenaged mom and dropped out of high school, as well. She also began to drink and our relationship would forever change. My mother's nephew, Perry, later moved in with us, and we had a house full of dysfunction.

I remember I was nine years old when my father let Johnathan, then 12, come visit for the summer. I was so excited. I finally got to meet my older brother who was tall and slim and looked more like my sibling than anyone else. I'd planned to show him the big city! I remember taking him to 42nd street so he could play all the arcade games his heart desired. My father would eventually let Johnathan stay in New York to attend school, so my mother finally had all four of her children under one roof.

My mother and I doted on Johnathan and he could do no wrong.

Not until he started trying to hang with Kenny and Sonya, and started drinking and coming home wasted. My mother told him he had to go back down south and return to our father. I guess she was afraid he'd end up like my other siblings. Later, Johnathan would say to her, "you don't know what's happening to your son in North Carolina." It was a long time before I truly understood what he meant.

My siblings moved from drinking to drugs and our house became known as the "crack" house. I can recall ten crack heads all under one roof. My mother continued to work two jobs to keep a roof over our heads and by now, I started to resent my mother and often blamed her for not putting her foot down and kicking my brother and the rest of the crack heads out.

Joe Plumber, who had moved in with us, also became a nightmare, drinking and making sexual advances towards my sister and other women in the house, yet my mother still allowed this man to live with us. I often wondered, as hard as my mother worked, how could she just allow my siblings to steal and sell things around the house and not get mad or frustrated? I remember going to make a phone call and the phone was gone, or looking up at the wall to see what time it was and the clock was gone. My mother even hid her purse in my room in the ceiling to try and keep it safe. This was our normal, this was my life.

I remember being in 5th grade and my brother Kenny dropped me on my head and my shoulder came down on the side of the bed rail. I had to go to the ER and my shoulder was in a sling for a few days. I called 911 and wanted to press charges against him. The cops were called to our home often and they always told me if anyone hurt me to call 911 and press charges. I missed a lot of school and my teacher, Mrs. Kornegay inquired about what was going on at home. I told her about what took place in our home and she told me, "that's your mother's son, and she will never kick him out." Those words would sit with me for a very long time.

I remember being at the courthouse and my mother threatening to put me in a home if I did not drop the charges against my brother Kenny. I refused. I knew our situation was not right and since she wouldn't do something about it, I decided I would. I don't know what finally happened, but I remember going into a phone booth, calling my grandma Remel, and telling her my mother had threatened to put me in a home. I was never sent to a home and I don't think my brother was ever charged with anything.

Still, at only ten years old, I was fully prepared to stick up for myself, even if my mother wasn't willing to have my back. It didn't matter to me. I knew right from wrong and what was going on in our house was wrong.

Because our house was 'that house,' with a bullet hole in the front door, I constantly stayed in the streets. I'd often cut school and stay out just before my mother was scheduled to come home from work. I'd get home about 6:00 AM and she'd arrive home around 7:30 AM. I was in middle school and very independent. My sister was pregnant with her second child, and her live-in boyfriend was on drugs too.

I don't recall speaking to my mother a lot. I tried to avoid her and everyone in the house as much as possible. I'd talk to my mother when I wanted money to buy the latest reeboks or jewelry. If we did have conversations, it was always me yelling at her about why Joe Plumber was still around and why couldn't she just stop taking care of my drug-addicted siblings. If it was just the two of us, things would be fine. She wouldn't have to work so hard and nothing would go missing.

I continued to spend more and more time in the streets, often hooking up with different neighborhood friends and going all over Brooklyn. Because I was tall, people often thought I was older than I was and most of my friends were as much as four years older than me. I sought out big sisters, best friends, uncles, and even aunts. It was nothing for me to call someone else's Grandma, Grandma, or if one of my friends had an aunt, she became my aunt. I was trying to create family member roles that did not exist in my own family.

As I look back on those days, I now realize my mother noticed I gravitated more and more to other people's families and wanted less to do with my own family. My mother longed for her children to be close to each other, and she provided us with many of the things that she did not have growing up. I never really saw my mother with close family members. I knew she had a brother who had died, and I learned of a cousin who also died, just before she and my mother were supposed to go off to nursing school together. Cousin Mary remained, and my mother was always excited to see her. Mary drove a car and dropped into town every so often, and we knew that would put a smile on my mother's face. However, those visits were infrequent. So much more of our time was dominated by dysfunction and chaos.

I remember going home around 2:00 AM one morning and my house was lit. We probably had about ten crack heads living in our home, including tenants, siblings, my mother's only nephew, and his girlfriend. There was no way I was going to get any sleep, so I just went to the park of P.S. 289 and swung on the swing until I got tired. I was scared because I remember hearing about a rapist who was snatching little girls and killing them. To this day I don't know if I went to that park with a gun or a knife. I remember having a weapon and saying out loud, "I don't think you want to mess with me," when I heard someone lurking. I just kept swinging on that swing, going higher and higher, doing tricks I'd normally be scared to do, just trying to wait it out, until I could go home and all the noise was silenced. For some reason, crackheads stayed up all night.

When I was in 7th grade, we had a house fire. To this day, I don't know how the fire started, but I believe this is when my mother started planning to relocate us from New York to North Carolina. When she spoke of these plans, I was absolutely devastated and blamed my siblings because I thought my mother was trying to escape the crack epidemic. I explained to her that crack was everywhere and I knew friends who would travel to North Carolina to sell crack and it was more expensive. That if they were stealing now, it would only get worse in North Carolina. I could not believe she wanted to ruin my life and move us to North Carolina because my brother and sister were on drugs. How could she always put them before me? I did not do drugs, I didn't drink, and I had not dropped out of school.

One day during the summer of 1989, I went into my mother's room to ask her for money to buy a new pair of sandals.

She jokingly said, "you won't need sandals because next week you can walk in the dirt!"

I was confused and asked what she was talking about. She said with such excitement that she'd purchased a house in North

Carolina and we were moving to Raeford, North Carolina the very next week. I think I had a mini-meltdown. Granted, half of our furniture was already gone, and she'd been cleaning out the house for what felt like years after the fire.

I put up such a fuss, that my mother allowed me to stay in New York with her while she finalized things before the move. My sister, my two nephews, and our maternal grandmother Nana relocated to Raeford, North Carolina. My mother and I stayed in New York until October and I was able to start Boys and Girls High School. You couldn't tell me my life wasn't about to begin.

My mother's nephew, Perry, loaded up the U-Haul and packed up all of our remaining things from Lincoln Place. We headed down 95 south to Raeford. We were moving into a single-family rancher my mother purchased in her hometown. For a while, things seemed normal. There were no regular phone calls to 911, my brother remained in New York and my sister sat still while pregnant with her 3rd son. Things seemed normal and I remember asking my mom, "How come I see you so often now?"

She responded, "Because I have one job now."

Although she was home more often, I can't say that she was more present than our life in New York.

My brother Johnathan came to live with us in Raeford. He was 17 now and could drive to see us whenever he pleased. So, Johnathan returned and having my brother around was great! He taught me how to drive and he made me practice completing a 3 point turn on every side road we passed. I still think I can pop a 3-point turn in the middle of anywhere because my brother taught me how.

One night while lying in bed watching TV, my brother was bent down on the side of my bed watching TV with me. All of a sudden, I felt his hand touch my leg. I jumped and said, "what are you doing?" His touch felt awkward and I didn't understand. When I told my mother what happened, she asked Johnathan about it and he said he was looking for the remote control. Although I didn't believe him, it sounded like the only logical explanation. Why would my brother try to touch my leg?

I took Johnathan to parties with me and even tried to hook him up with one of my friends. He'd get comfortable with us in Raeford, then up and leave and return to Franklinton with Fred. We didn't realize he was being hospitalized and had been diagnosed with schizophrenia.

Johnathan's behavior continued to change and make me feel uncomfortable. At this point, I threw myself into Track and Field and Cross Country. He'd look at me weird and I'd go run 3 miles. One day my mother asked my sister what was wrong with me, and my sister yelled out, "Your son keeps looking at her inappropriately!" By this time, he'd asked me to have sex with him. I knew it was wrong and something a brother should never ask his sister. I thought maybe he was asking whether I would have sex with him if I weren't his sister. My mother stopped asking him about the instances I mentioned to her. It's like she shut down and did not want to discuss it anymore.

Then one night while trying on my prom dress, Johnathan gave me this look I will never forget. I ran off and went into my room and began to cry. My mother would not help, so I contacted Mr. Raynor, a social worker I trusted, from my middle school. I told him that my brother was looking at me funny, asked me to have sex with him and I continued to tell him the strange things that would go on in my house. Mr. Rayor warned me that my brother was going to try and rape me, and I should get out of the house immediately. My mother begged Johnathan to get help. I remember him lifting her off the floor by her neck in anger, refusing to get treatment. Thankfully, Joe Plumber was there and he was able to get Johnathan to let my mother go. I stayed a couple of nights at my sister's house, but she was back on drugs and her house reminded me a lot of our house in New York; it was never still or quiet, and people were going in and out all night. Staying at her house was short-lived and I returned home. Johnathan briefly went to stay with Fred, and then returned to Raeford with us.

As a senior in High School, all I could think about was winning the State Championship in Track & Field and going off to college on a scholarship. Division I schools were interested in me and I had taken the S.A.T a few times. All I had to do was finish my senior year, and then I'd be able to escape my mother's house. Things seemed promising.

On Wednesday, April 21, 1993, I'd returned home from a track meet. My mother had gone to work – she worked 3rd shift now. Joe Plumber left to go to New York, and my high school boyfriend was off visiting New York as well. Within hours of returning home, Johnathan and I were in the house alone.

I began to undress to shower and soak. I'd run hard and my body was feeling the pain. The phone rang and I began an hour-long conversation with my friend from New York. As our conversation wrapped up, my boyfriend beeped in on call waiting and I took his call. At this point, getting in the tub was no longer an option, so I decided I would go in my bedroom and just talk to him, and soak later.

When I entered my room, Johnathan was there waiting for me. My boyfriend started yelling for me to tell him to get out of my room. Johnathan knew he shouldn't be there. My mother had instructed him to stay away from me, and he wasn't allowed in my bedroom. His response was only "make me get out," and he began to attack me. The phone fell from my hands and he began ripping my clothes off and trying to have sex with me. He punched me in my side and said, "you know how to do this" and continued to try and insert his penis into my vagina. I begged for him to stop. I promised him I wouldn't tell anyone if he'd just let me go.

Suddenly there was a knock at the front door. It would not stop and he jumped up off of me. I immediately jumped up to run behind him. He drew back his fist and said, "put some clothes on" as he went to the front door. I grabbed the nearest pair of pants and a t-shirt and ran as fast as I could out the back door. I jumped the fence, ran to a neighbor's house, and started banging on the door. I was crying and bloody and explained that my brother tried to rape me. My neighbor called 911, and then we realized 911 was already at my house. What I didn't realize was my boyfriend had been on the phone listening almost the entire time. He finally hung up and had someone call the police. The police arrived at the neighbor's house and I shared exactly what happened. They could tell from the room being a mess that a struggle took place and they arrested my brother.

From the police station, we called my mother. I remember her crying and saying she did not want to hear what happened. She was going to lose everything. How would she get him out of jail? My heart just sank. What about me? My brother just tried to rape me!

When I returned home, I called my father and told him what happened. He told me I was a liar and his boy would never do anything like that. He also mentioned that my older sister said he touched her once and women lie all the time and hung up on me. I remember sliding down the wall with the phone in my hand thinking, but what about me? I'm not lying. He really just did this to me! I later took a shower and just scrubbed my body and kept trying to wash it all away. In the back of my mind thinking, but you need to go to the hospital to get a rape kit done. So that's what I did. I asked my neighbor to take me to the hospital to get a rape kit. My mother did not go with me, I don't remember her ever mentioning anything.

When the nurse asked me what happened, I said, "My brother tried to rape me." The look on that Nurse's face is one I will never forget. When I arrived home, I was too distraught to sleep in my bed, so I slept with my mother that night. She didn't hold me, she didn't tell me everything would be alright. I think I cried all night, and so did she. I did not go to school Thursday or Friday, I missed my Senior Prom on Saturday, and Monday I returned to school like nothing happened. My lip was still swollen and I could still feel the knots on my head.

My brother never came back home. My mother never discussed what happened, and my anger towards her began to boil over. I was the only child who did not drop out of high school. I wasn't a teen mom, and I wasn't addicted to drugs and alcohol. But her schizophrenic son tried to rape me, and I'm just out here to fend for myself. His mother and father had his back. Not mine. My mother raised me, but did she even love me? How could my mother, the only parent that raised me, not have my back?

I'd later graduate high school, earn Female Athlete of the Year, and win the State Championship at 800 meters. I was awarded an athletic grant and aid to UNC- Wilmington along with my best friend Michael. While at UNC-Wilmington I began to suffer from PTSD. I started to have flashbacks and I would black out. I remember getting a call from my brother's attorney. My mother was paying for his attorney, while sending me $20, a book of stamps, and a check to cover the difference in tuition.

During this time, I also started researching sexual abuse and mental illness. I'd come to the realization that my mother must have suffered from some kind of sexual abuse. I learned that when victims did not heal, they weren't able to help others, and that included their children. I started to come to terms with the fact that mental illness ran in my family, yet no one discussed it; I was determined to change that. Later my PTSD caused me to leave college and my dreams of participating in the 1996 Olympics were gone. I remember crying and crying and thinking, he took so much from me, but I would not let him take anything else. I was determined to heal from this awful experience. However, my mother did not make it easy. When I returned home from college she called me a college drop-out and handed me my car note and car insurance. I only had $200 saved under my mattress and now I needed to find a job.

Just as I was starting to forgive my mother, pain and anger festered and bubbled up inside me again. She blamed me for Johnathan going to jail. I found a letter she had written to her cousin

Mary describing her anger that he had attacked me (without any mention of rape), and it was up to me what the prosecutor would do. I remember crying and yelling at her, telling her he did not attack me, he tried to rape me. "Your son tried to have sex with your daughter!" I believed my brother suffered from mental illness, but I also believed he knew what he did. When he drew back his fist and told me to put on clothes, when he told my mother to tell me to say, "we just had a fight," he proved that he knew what he did to me was wrong. I knew my mother was sick, too, but it did not matter. Not taking my side, not standing up for me, hurt, and hurt like hell.

I returned home and refused to live with her, I stayed with friends and worked full time and did not return to school right away. As I continued to heal and better understand why my mother did not fight for me, I began to visit her more often, never talking about the sexual assault or mentioning my brother. As much as I wanted her to pick me, I knew my mother would never abandon any of her children. I recalled what my 5th-grade teacher, Ms. Kornegay said: "That's your mother's son, and she will never put him out." I had to come to terms with the fact that my mother loved me, but because she was broken and never healed, she would never be able to show up for me and I knew deep down in my heart she never would.

I eventually returned home and my mother gave me a room on the far end of the house that had its own entrance. I began working full time and attending school full time. Later my mother would give me a birthday card for my birthday – the very same birthday card – two years in a row. I'll never forget the words printed in that card:

*"Many of the choices you've had to make have been more difficult than those I faced when I was your age. I haven't always agreed with your decisions, but I hope you know that I respect your courage and independence in making them. You're doing all you can to be the person you want to be, and I admire that..."*

I felt like, in my mother's own way, she was applauding me for standing up to her, and standing alone in what her son did to me. She was apologizing in the only way she knew how. She was letting me know that she loved me.

One early morning in October 1998, my sister Sonya came running in my bedroom. "It's Mommy, it's Mommy, I think she had a stroke!" I rushed to my mother's room. She was leaned over to one side, not speaking and looked in a daze. We rushed her to the hospital. I remember she was lying on a stretcher in the ER when she started yelling, "Wendy! Where's Wendy! Where's Wendy?!?" And I said, "I'm right here, Mommy, I'm right here."

That is the last time, I remember my mother saying my name in her clear voice. When they admitted her to the hospital she cried, and we all began to cry in her hospital room. My sister Sonya was devastated. I would soon realize this event would change our lives forever.

In the year that followed, doctors would find colon cancer and perform surgery to remove a large mass from my mother's abdomen. I was now the head of the household, paying all the bills my mother's disability check did not cover. Initially, I worked a telemarketing job earning $7.75 an hour. It was the perfect job for a college student, but with my mother sick, I was unable to return to school. I had to take care of my mother.

I remember clearly one night I'd worked overtime and arrived home in the wee hours of the morning. My mother's feeding machine beeped loudly and rang throughout the entire house. I went in her room, changed her sheets, washed her up, and changed her milk. I kissed her on her forehead and told her I loved her. I went back to my room and cried. I wanted to tell my mother I was sorry for being so angry with her most of my life. That I understood how much she loved all four of her children, and how hard it must have been for her to feel like she needed to pick a side. I wanted her to know I forgave her. I wanted her to know I understood her.

At that moment, I knew just how much I loved my mother because nothing else mattered. I needed to get a better job, so I could take better care of her. I wasn't worried about finishing college. I understood the sacrifices my mother made having children in her late 30's, sending us to private school, purchasing a first home, a second home, and working two jobs most of my life. It all made sense and I wasn't angry anymore. I made it my mission to tell my mother how sorry I was, and that I no longer blamed her.

I never got that chance. The next day, I got a call at work that my mother was breathing funny and it didn't sound normal. I rushed to the hospital, and immediately, we were met by a Chaplain. I remember telling him to get away from me, that they were going to drain the fluid from my mother's lungs and we were going to take her home in a few days.

The doctor told me they were going to insert a tube in my

mother's throat to help her breathe. My mother sucked her teeth and rolled her eyes at me. She was a long- term care nurse and understood everything that was happening. She knew she was dying. Another doctor approached me and told me how sick my mother was, and that she'd likely not survive surgery. He told me to think about her quality of life. Quality of life. That statement echoed in the air for what seemed like forever and kept repeating itself: think about her quality of life.

I remember standing in the hallway, seeing what looked like a scene out of an episode of a medical drama, and yelling at the top of my lungs, "STOP! Just Stop! Let her go! " I'd just given the hospital staff permission to let my mother die. I heard a long beep which seemed to go on forever. Hazel Mae Finkley succumbed to her illness on August 29, 2000, at approximately 2:38 AM.

Ten years after my sexual assault, I served as a volunteer 24-hour Emergency Room Responder. I held victims' hands in the emergency room while nurses administered rape kits. Later that same year, I walked across the stage, graduating with my Bachelor of Science Degree in Mass Communications with a concentration in Broadcast Journalism. I remember arriving at the ceremony and one of my classmates said, "I prayed for you this morning. You were on my mind." I immediately began to cry.

I cried because I missed my mom and I hoped I finally made her proud; I wasn't a college drop-out. I finished. It took me ten years, but I never gave up. I forgave my mom, but it would take me another six years before I forgave myself.

# Healing My Hungry Heart

*By Renetta D. Weaver*

*A touch of forgiveness feels like love. The warmth of
forgiveness heals all wounds. Forgiveness recalibrates
the compass for the relationship with oneself and others.*

O n a hot summer night in 1970, with a violent collision of sperm
and egg, I was conceived, and for the next nine months I
was nestled inside the womb of my teenaged birth mom's petite
frame. I imagine as a pregnant teen, she was overwhelmed with
carrying the weight of being inadequately prepared to manage
the flood of hormones that naturally accompany puberty and her
unplanned pregnancy.

Given the initial framework of my life, I imagine I floated with
the grace of an Olympic swimmer in an amniotic abyss of toxic
stress, anxiety, and trauma. I was baptized daily in the secrecy of
my birth mother's womb. Most likely my mother ate and nourished
me with non-sustainable meals that were bathed in a broth of guilt
and shame, and seasoned with silence. Borrowing from one of the
slogans of the 12-step community, "we're as sick as our secrets," and

so I suppose I was unwell from my inception. My life was rooted in secrecy, and my young, unwed, pregnant mother was sent away from her home to ensure that.

In April 1971, my teenaged mother gave birth to me in an unknown, all-girls home. Immediately following my delivery, I was taken and placed in the custody of Social Services, where I was tagged with a code name, photographed, and marketed for advertisement to families with just a little more room in their hearts for one more child. For my first three months, I lived in the purgatory known as foster care.

After this, I was placed for adoption with my forever family. Before the 1980's, all formal adoptions were closed to protect the privacy rights of the birth mother.

Consequently, the records of my birth process and adoption were made private, marked with a seal and filed away in the vault of the County Court House. Another layer of secrecy.

In her letter to my family, my foster mom described me as a good baby who was on schedule with sleeping and eating, but my forever mom said she lied because all I did as a baby was cry. I'll never get to verify that story because my foster mother's name was crossed out in the letter – her identity another secret. My forever mom told me that my foster mom scratched out her own name, and although I have my doubts, I have no choice but to accept and forgive it. This cycle of acceptance and forgiveness has been a lifelong theme for me.

I grew up with a lot of family secrets and emotional longing. Secrets like the ones I was implanted and rooted in, and longing for connection. Because I was not born in a hospital and my birth records were sealed, I always felt like a book with a missing chapter. There are a lot of people who know about that secret part of my life. But I always felt like there was no one I could communicate with about these things.

My adoptive mother made me feel that I was wrong to express anything personal, and when I did, I was made to feel guilt and shame. Mama's word was law, and breaking it had consequences. So I began stuffing my feelings. Stuffing my hurt, my guilt, stuffing my loneliness and frustration, and stuffing my shame led to stuffing my body with food.

I carried 250 pounds of those emotions on my body.

My story explores how emotional hunger and the weight of unforgiveness played a major role in my weight gain, and how forgiveness factored into me achieving a new body, mind, and spirit for living life.

Whenever I smell Vicks Vapor rub, or see its label, it warms and comforts me, because it reminds me of the times when I felt closest to my mother. I can still remember being a little 6-year-old girl, lying in my bed with a cold, as my mother sat beside me and rubbed that medicine on my chest. I do not know if it was the vapor rub that helped me feel better or if it was the love and affection that I felt from my mother's hands that really healed me. Either way, when I close my eyes and allow myself to imagine a time that I felt my mother's love the most, it is always the memory of her soothing hands on my chest.

That experience is likely the foundation for my love language, which is physical touch. I am a hugger and find physical affection a natural expression of my feelings.

However, when I go to hug my mom, I cannot seem to grasp the intimacy I once felt between us. Instead, it always feels like I can never capture that initial sensation of love and affection. My brain never forgot how good it felt when my mother touched me, and I learned early that touch felt like love.

I can remember when I stopped feeling my mother's affection. It happened when the trials of life stole her attention. Like a drug addict, when I was no longer getting that stimulation from my mother, I started chasing and trying to capture that feeling through other forms of physical touch.

I can remember when I started wearing a mask to cover up the pain that I was feeling. The mask looked like a big smile and seemed to work because no one ever asked me whether I was ok. People used to say, "You're always smiling" and I would just smile harder. I am certain this is the reason people seem to ignore me.

This is so ironic, because although I did not necessarily want to be seen, I still wanted to be acknowledged. For most of my life, I felt lonely and invisible and hidden from the person I wanted most to see me, and that was my mother.

My mom was also the mom of my two teenaged older brothers, and the wife of a first generation college graduate with whom she migrated up North for better career opportunities. She was a woman who put her own aspirations on the back burner to ensure that we were all ok.

Without the support of her parents and our extended family, she had her hands full with trying to keep us all together in this new middle class lifestyle and neighborhood. All of the neighborhood boys, including my brothers, fell into the teenage behaviors of drinking alcohol, smoking marijuana, and having sex.

For the most part, I was quiet and unassuming, not because I was so good but because I was paralyzed with shyness, and I suffered from social anxiety. I would cling to my mother, and rarely allowed her to go anywhere without me. She tried to do things like put me in tap, ballet, and cheerleading but when it came time to perform, I would always quit. I know this was disappointing to her because she did not understand why her little girl could not be like other little girls. I did not know how to explain to her that I just did not feel confident being seen and I only felt safe when I was with her.

My mom and I continued to be close until I was about eight years old. One day my babysitter told me that I needed to go straight home. My babysitter lived just a few houses up the street from me so it was not strange to walk home by myself. However, it was strange for me to be sent home so early. When I arrived home and entered the door, I curiously walked up the steps. My mom greeted me in tears and told me that her mom, my granny, had died. We packed our bags and flew to Florida to attend her funeral.

I remember going to the wake to view my grandmother's body and just staring at her face. I felt like I could see her still moving and breathing but she was gone forever. Burying my grandmother was very painful for my mom, and witnessing this whole process was very confusing for me. I had so many questions, but I never asked them, and no one ever asked me how I felt.

After returning home things were never the same. At my grandmother's funeral, I had witnessed my mother's visible sorrow and pain. However, when we returned home it seemed like my mother became emotionally and physically distant. I felt like I wanted to comfort her but I did not know how. I also did not know how to tell her that I was lonely and needed comforting. I can only assume that being consumed with profound sadness from mourning the death of her mother left her with the inability to share her heart in the manner that she used to.

It was shortly after this time that I had been telling my mother that my friend was adopted. That led to her revealing to me the truth about my own adoption. It happened casually, as she was combing my hair, but I was devastated by the revelation. I only vaguely remember running out of the house to our unlocked car in the driveway. I sat in the front seat of our Pinto Station Wagon, and sobbed.

After that day, I started to "act-out" until my mother had enough of my misbehavior. She said to me, "Look, you are no different than your brothers and I will spank you like I spank them." That actually made me feel like my mother still loved me, and I learned that there were other physical expressions of love. The hugs and gentle touches that I used to get from her were being replaced with spankings. And I accepted them as a substitute for her long-remembered loving touch.

I continued to grow physically, but I was emotionally stuck. I missed the intimacy I used to feel from my mother. I was starving for connection and belonging. I remember one of my friends spent the night, and she taught me to play doctor. The things we did felt good, but my mother scolded and shamed me, and that's when I learned that while touch felt very good, I was bad for allowing it to happen.

When I was nine, my parents became consumed with trying

to figure out what to do about my brothers, who started getting into trouble with truancy, weed, and alcohol. It was scary with so much chaos in my home. From hearing my parents argue with my brothers and each other to my brothers leaving home, I became lonely. It was like I was invisible because no one was talking to me. I wanted to show affection to my mother when she was crying, but I didn't know how. I felt pushed away.

My heart hunger surfaced, and my older brother's teenaged friend, who frequented my home and called my mother "moms," noticed it. He groomed me by catching me upstairs playing by myself and telling me how pretty and mature I was. He eventually sexually molested me in my house and later in his house.

My self-confidence eroded rapidly. I felt like I was bad and like I did something bad. I did not tell anyone what happened, not even my mom. All of my relationships in my teen and adult years mirrored the experience of rejection and disconnection that I felt with my mom, and the loss of self-esteem from the sexual abuse I suffered. I seemed to chase and fall in love with people who were detached and emotionally unavailable. I eventually ended up in repeated relationships that included substance abuse, as well as verbal and physical abuse. At the same time, I started eating my trauma and emotions by choking down food and sleeping a lot. I fell in love with the escape that sugar, salt, and fat provided me. French fries, bacon, and pizza became my best friends.

That lack of emotional connection with my mother left me feeling unwanted and rejected. I also felt abandoned by her when I needed someone to talk to throughout the years. I had this deep resentment and anger towards her, and a complete lack of faith in myself. I wanted her to express her love by telling me I was good enough. However, that just was not her way, so I never got the verbal affirmation I was seeking. Because of this, my internal dialogue was full of self-hatred and criticism.

I experienced so many cycles of failed relationships, and fruitless, damaging, sexual behaviors, some of which left me with permanent physical scars, and loss of fertility. And I continued to struggle desperately with obesity. So I started looking for answers. I wanted to know how to overcome my anger, depression, and suicidal thoughts. I wanted to find the secret to being happy and at peace. I began looking inward and in my search, I discovered that my relationship with my mother was at the root of how I saw my relationships, the world and myself. In an attempt to heal our relationship, I asked her to go to therapy with me. She was not down with that plan at all so I was left with one of two choices. Either face everything and recover, or forget everything and run. Well after years of running from person to place to try to fill a void, I knew that I had to face everything. And I knew I needed medical help to overcome my obesity.

In 2016, I had to have a psychological evaluation before I could receive the final approval from my insurance company for bariatric surgery. This was required to ensure that I addressed any mental health or psychological conditions that were contributing to my weight. I can remember feeling extremely nervous as I sat across from my evaluator. For the past 20 years, I have spent my career in social work interviewing and evaluating countless numbers of individuals. Although I never felt like I was judging my clients, this time felt different because I was not sitting in the position of power.

I was the one being interviewed and my verbal and non-verbal responses evaluated. That alone made me feel vulnerable, and like I was going to be judged by someone else who could see the real me. I started formulating in my mind how I planned to answer the psychologist's questions. I knew I could no longer pretend I was without issues, but I did not want my approval for surgery to be declined because I was too emotional.

After my evaluation, the psychologist told me that I was a great candidate for bariatric surgery, but he cautioned me that I was going to have to figure out how to manage my overall life without stuffing my emotions with food. I already knew that most weight loss surgery patients regain their weight and it is not because they did not try hard enough or do not have enough willpower to control their eating. I knew from my own experience that it is easy to be successful at losing the weight, but hard to keep it off, even with all the knowledge and tools.

During weight loss surgery, part of the stomach is removed, which greatly reduces its production of the hunger hormone Ghrelin. The surgery results in the body not being as physically hungry, and the remaining stomach is so tiny that only small portions of food can be consumed at a time.

What I quickly discovered is that the surgery did not remove my head and heart hunger. This was an insatiable hunger connected to feelings of pain tied to experiences in that past that I had not forgiven.

When I started going on my personal journey of healing I constantly heard that forgiveness is not for the other person, but for myself. I wanted to forgive my mother, but I felt like I could not release her until she acknowledged her role in my hurt. Our problem was that she felt the same way. She felt hurt and rejected by me and I would not acknowledge it. I did not feel like I had done anything wrong, but merely protected myself from her. And she was protecting herself from me. Therefore, we were both walking around wounded waiting for the other to make it right. Furthermore, we did not have the appropriate words to express what we needed from each other.

I could get into all our petty arguments, but at the end of the day that is what they were. Instead of truly sitting down and communicating, we just kept sweeping feelings and conflict under the rug, and getting hurt every time we tripped.

Recently my mom said, "I do not know why you hate me so much. Everything I say you take offense to it."

I was stunned and realized that she really did not understand why I was upset. I also began to understand that she really did not do anything intentionally to upset me. That is when I felt the most saddened because I discovered that I had been holding out for something that I was never going to get from my mama. Not because she would not have done anything for me but because she just did not get it nor get me.

In the past few years, I started understanding that she was not just my mom she was a person too. When I began viewing her as a woman, I started seeing her humanity. I could relate to her thoughts, feelings, and vulnerabilities. I began to understand that she had been emotionally guarded most of my life, and that became a barrier in our relationship. Having experienced the same reaction in response to being hurt, I could now understand my mom with a new mindset.

My mom and I felt misunderstood by one another plenty of times. We carried our pasts with us and added it to each new experience. The cycle of anger, resentment, and hurt multiplied. Every time we felt those toxic emotions, our brains shut down our ability to think rationally, so we both continued to respond with hurt. I started realizing I could restore the harmony in our relationship by choosing not to allow my emotions to take over. This started changing the dynamic of our relationship.

I started to realize that I needed certain things from my mom that she could not give me because she did not have it to give. When I accepted her as she was, I could begin to appreciate her and stop fighting. Even if she did not change, I needed to.

Because of childhood trauma and being adopted, I felt different and developed an identity of shame. I did not get the acceptance in the way that I needed from my mother and used to beat myself up for not feeling good enough. When I started extending grace upon myself by using positive self-talk and speaking positive affirmations, I was able to rewire the negative mental scripts that were unconsciously playing in my head.

Now that I love myself, it is easy to let go toxic relationships with others because I no longer need anyone outside of me to make me feel good enough. My relationship with my mother is still a work in progress. I am doing my part by working on being the change I want to see. I am beginning to extend grace to my mother, others, and myself.

I am not perfect, and those old habits of being guarded and defensive still hijack my responses when I feel that my mother is being distant and critical. However, what I have discovered is that when I do move towards grace it always ends up benefiting me. When I do move in the direction of grace I remind myself of the following consequences:

- When I was in that space of unforgiveness towards myself and my mother I developed this pattern of emotional eating, I gained weight, I felt depressed and I was always feeling sick to my stomach or experiencing some kind of pain in my body.

- When I was holding on to anger it was blocking me from experiencing the fullness of joy in my other relationships. My unconscious thoughts held onto past images of hurt and mistrust. I was constantly on guard looking out for anything that resembled a threat from others. When I was guarded it made it difficult to form healthy intimate relationships because I kept people from getting close.

- When I was not living in a space of forgiveness, I missed the opportunity to get past my past and experience new beginnings. Unforgiveness felt like the annoyance of having a pebble in my shoe. Every time I tried to move forward, I just feel it irritated. I tried to shift it around and ignore it yet that feeling was still there. Eventually I had to stop and take the pebble out in order to get ahead.

Letting go was not easy because I had this victim narrative that I was playing on repeat. I did not want to let it go because I would use it to validate my anger. I would say to myself: "My mother was supposed to do this, or my mother should not have done that." As I began to deal with my unsuccessful weight loss issues I had to come to terms that I was holding on to the armor that I had been using to hide the anger and unforgiveness towards my mother. I had to realize that I could not successfully lose the weight without letting go of my resentment towards the past.

There was a payoff for my resentment and I used that to justify why I could not trust women, why I ate every time I felt any emotion and why I could not show up in my life. The honest question I had to ask myself was, "Do I want to be right or do I want to win?" When I laid down on the table to have weight loss surgery, I knew I was ready to win.

I have to reiterate that forgiveness has not been an easy journey for me because it meant that I had to let go of the fantasy that I had of my mother. Although she did not express love in the way that I longed for I had to appreciate and accept that she really did love me. Letting go of our fantasy relationship has truly been a grieving process but the new relationship we are developing gives me hope. Forgiveness has been the missing ingredient to my emotional peace and my weight loss. Forgiveness has also improved my relationship with my mother by giving us the opportunity to rewrite our story as we discover a new normal.

One of the most pivotal healing moments in our relationship occurred when I wrote my first anthology chapter. I nervously hit send on my chapter and forwarded it to mama for her to read. Although I did not know how she was going to react, I imagined the worst based on our history. Surprisingly, after reading my chapter, my mother was mostly supportive in her better than best way. She commended me on my work, went on a cruise with me to see me launch the book, and was the first to purchase her copy. Looking into the audience and seeing my mama's face beam with pride was one of the most affirming moments of my life. Her reaction and actions felt like love.

My need for friendship, family and intimacy were factors in my ability to develop a healthy self-esteem, confidence and respect for others and myself. Forgiveness is allowing me to become my best self, which involves living freely, and expressing my creativity. Overall what I have learned by reflecting on the relationship between my mother and me is that, the touch of forgiveness feels like love, the warmth of forgiveness heals all wounds, and forgiveness recalibrates the compass for my relationship with myself and others.

In this process of forgiveness, I embraced a few concepts that you might find helpful:

- Forgiveness is a choice and if you are not ready to forgive it is your choice not to.
- Forgiveness is a journey, not an event, so it is important to be patient with the process.
- Forgiveness is an act, not an emotion, therefore no matter how you feel you can let go.

My mother always said, "Give me my flowers while I am here to smell them." By choosing to let go of the past, I am extending this olive branch while she is still here to receive it.

# Breaking Chains One Link at a Time

*By Sonia James*

"Honey, they left the baby at the hospital!"

"So, what are you going to do?" Auntie asked.

"I guess I'm going to get the baby," Grandma replied."

I can hear the conversation as if I had dialed in on three-way. To have the story told to me as an adult was hilarious. In actuality, it was no laughing matter and could have been a serious situation. But I have to admit, I chuckled when Auntie recounted the story, probably because of the way she told it, with love and the perspective of years.

It was a Saturday and I had promised to bring Auntie breakfast and give her a facial, but I wound up staying the entire day. Auntie is my grandma's oldest living sibling on my father's side of the family. She remembered the details because she was there, and she took her time recalling them.

She began by asking me, "Has anyone ever told you about how you got home from the hospital?" She had my undivided attention from that point on. I was like a five-year-old being read a story. I took it all in. I didn't want that day to end – the stories, the laughter, and even the tears. To hear how my life began was invigorating. Still, so many questions, and answers I didn't think I'd ever get. I shared with Auntie how for years I felt like I didn't fit in, and didn't feel like a legitimate member of the family.

Neither my grandmother nor anyone in the family ever made me feel unwelcomed. But the story Auntie told me proved that neither of my parents was ready for a baby. My grandmas on both sides – my mother's mom and my father's mom – stepped in and picked up where my mother and father did not or could not. But even two loving grandmothers could not fill in every gap in my childhood, or protect me from all the hurt and deep sadness that followed me.

We were a family that harbored secrets, and secrets never unfold at the right time, if ever there is a right time. The catchphrase 'it ain't where you from, it's where you at' is a lie. I am grown now so I can say lie. Lie! Lie! Lie! To say lie growing up in our house was just as bad as cursing. But by keeping secrets, the adults in my family were telling lies of omission and setting the children up for dysfunction.

I remember being at a family reunion when an older cousin asked if my father and I had the same last name. I said yes, believing it to be true. I was eight at that time, but it was years later before I learned my last name was not the same as my father's. I had no clue. How could I not know my father's last name was different from mine? I don't remember ever having a conversation with my mother about my father. And so I began to understand how hard my family worked to harbor secrets. They even kept secrets from me about myself!

Growing up I understood so little about my father's life. I believed my father's family had money, lived in nice houses, took trips and vacations, and had family reunions. This wasn't my experience, and so I began to feel I didn't fit in. I also began distancing myself from others, which only made my tendency to self-sabotage worse.

Don't get it twisted, I had a place to lay my head and food to eat. I never went to bed hungry. I always had a coat in the winter and a new dress at Easter. There was always lunch at school, even if sometimes it was a free lunch. Both grandmas made sure I had what I needed.

My immediate family consisted of my grandmother, my two uncles, my sister, and until I was eleven or twelve, my mother. There were times when my mother would go away for days, sometimes months, and at one point for almost a year, if not longer. Her absences always seemed like an eternity.

Home for me was always different from my friends' homes. I didn't know just how different until my teenage years. Friends rarely came to my house. If they did, we talked at the front door or I'd make an excuse to go to their house instead. I never had sleepovers with friends at my house. And I felt shame in knowing we were different.

In my sophomore year of high school, life was forever changed when my grandmother, who was my support, my refuge, and my safety, died. And when she died, the family unit--and my small sense of stability--died with her. Grandma was only fifty-two.

My sisters and I were back and forth between my grandmother's house where my uncle now lived, and my stepfather's mother's house. It didn't help that my stepfather made it clear that I was not his, I was "that girl." I had nowhere to go. I was trapped.

My uncle didn't even like kids, and he made us feel unwelcome. This was the same uncle who would wake me out of bed when he was hungry. I was no gourmet chef, so cooking was simply putting a frozen pizza in the oven, something he could easily have done himself.

This was my life at 15. I had no voice. Saying no was not an option. Talking back was not an option either, unless I wanted the taste slapped out of my mouth. I learned early to be quiet and say nothing, but do as I was told. My grandmother was no longer there. And my mother was not around.

When my stepfather and mom moved into their own place, I moved in with them.

Our place outside of my school zone, so to avoid transferring schools, my only option was public transportation to and from high school. This was on my dime of course, so I was also working to afford what I needed. In fact, my wages paid our phone bill.

Working long hours gave me an escape and an opportunity to stay away from home as much as possible. Every now and then I could bum a ride either to or from work, but it was truly like pulling teeth to get my stepfather to give me a ride anywhere.

I also became a regular witness to my mother's suffering as a result of my stepfather's abuse. In addition to physical abuse, I became aware of his emotional abuse and total financial control of my mother. Because my mother didn't work and had to care for two toddlers at home, she was financially dependent upon my stepfather. I didn't have a driver's license and there was only one vehicle, so the wheels literally were put in motion to ensure I, too, was financially dependent upon him.

My mother was beautiful and fun. I remember we would get all dressed up for Easter, and head to the park or just have Easter egg hunts in the back yard. I am not sure when things changed, but leading up to the change in my mother's mental stability, if she wasn't working, she was at church, but it was one of those "holiness" churches where services lasted hours. My mom would take my sister and me to church all day Sunday for multiple services. Every Bible study we were there, every revival we were there. Loud music, tambourines, shouting, speaking in tongues—the only thing missing were the faith-testing snakes! It was a lot for a young person to comprehend. To my mother, it was religion... and fulfilling. To me, it was chilling.

During my high school years, I remember two specific events that further undermined my self-concept and punctuated the lack of support I experienced in my upbringing. First was my attempt to become a debutante. I remember vividly my white dress with ruffles and tiny, pink flowers, and my excitement as we drove in the old station wagon – filled with furniture, and a wall-sized painting that kept hitting the back of my seat – to the first meeting of hopeful girls and their mothers.

To my surprise, I discovered there would be panel interviews. I wasn't ready for questions, and especially not such thought-provoking questions. I needed preparation and time to practice, but I had no guidance at home. Bear in mind, no one in my family had been a debutante. I bombed the interview and bombed badly. I beat myself up for a while over that colossal failure. Too embarrassed to go back, I quit. I didn't participate in the fundraiser, so there was no Debutante Cotillion, no Deb Ball for me.

That same year, there were modeling tryouts for a school fashion show. After standing in line behind the auditorium stage curtains for what seemed like an eternity, it was my turn. I casually strolled across the stage in my normal walk. I wasn't selected because I was boring, and lacked the confidence and encouragement to strut across that stage with attitude. Perhaps if my family had been different, if I had a big brother or sister to look up to, or if I had a different mother, and a loving father in my life, I would have been more self-assured and projected more confidence. It seemed too late to matter.

There was no blueprint for surviving high school, no life template to follow. There were no birds and bees discussions. Sex education in our house amounted to a warning not to get pregnant, while being accused of being pregnant at the first sign of a cold or flu. By the time I was a senior in high school, I worked full-time hours. I learned the art of survival early on, so once again, it was just stay quiet and stay out of sight. Eventually, my mom began to distance herself from the church and her circle of church friends. Soon after leaving the church, I witnessed a shift in my mother's mental stability and several bouts of paranoia. She began to believe game show hosts were talking directly to her, and any laughter from the television was directed at her.

Without appropriate parents, there were no ground rules in our house, except the understanding that once you graduated high school, you were grown. And I could not wait. I survived high school and graduated, not because I was pushed to, but primarily because I completed the majority of the graduation requirements for an academic diploma during the first three years of high school.

College took a back seat. My stepfather refused to provide his information for my financial aid applications. Again, he was in control. The financial aid process was too overwhelming, and there was no one to explain other options, to encourage me, or to assure me that college was a must. And definitely, there was no one to pay for it.

I resented my mother and hated my stepfather. I started working extra shifts to earn more money and decided to buy myself a bed to replace the hideous canary yellow foam mattress that served as my bed on the floor of my bedroom. I picked out my bed and scheduled the delivery. But my stepfather turned the delivery men away at the front door. "Not in my house. You will not take over my house," he said.

He never missed an opportunity to remind me he was not my father and I was not his daughter. I had my own room but the room was bare. And my mother, increasingly unstable and distant, did nothing to help me. Not even to help me get my own bed.

Things at home continued to deteriorate, and finally, I reached the point where I simply could not take it anymore. My attempt at suicide was with sleeping pills. I don't know how many I swallowed. But I remember crying to my mom, who had called 911. I remember leaving by ambulance, throwing up and dry heaving uncontrollably on the ride to the nearest hospital. A doctor told my mom the pills were not strong enough to hurt me, only enough to make me sleep. Afterward, no one ever mentioned the incident or talked about it again.

I continued to work and was promoted to assistant manager, one of the youngest at the company. Money was good. And life was good. Love was good, too, so I thought. I met a guy, and after six months of dating, he asked me to marry him. I was the one. I was chosen.

In the beginning, I was mostly infatuated by his attention, and his desire to be with me every moment. Soon the need for attention erupted into something far from healthy. There were accusations – I smiled too much, made eye contact for too long, laughed too hard. What's really bizarre is it didn't matter if it was male, female, adult, or child – no one could have my attention. My young husband started showing up at my job unannounced, questioning the male voices in the background. Ignoring these incidents became a habit. Years passed and the insanity became customary.

From the outside looking in, my life was one to be envied. Masking the truth became my normal, just as it had been when I was a young girl. Once again, I was suffering in silence, smiling on the outside while hiding the shame on the inside. I was too embarrassed to ask for help. Surely his family knew about his temper; a cousin had a first-row seat to his violence, made worse by alcohol. I was becoming my mother!

My mom's disappearing acts were in full effect once again. This time there was no grandmother to step in. Days turned into weeks, and weeks turned into months, and it became clear she was not coming back home to take care of my little sisters.

Struggling through my growing pains, I did my best make sure my sisters were good. As the oldest, I felt it was my responsibility to do what was right for my baby sisters. It wasn't their fault. That was the turning point of my relationship with my stepdad. He recognized he needed help, and asked me for it. For the sake of my sisters, I put the past behind us and forgave him.

My adult relationship with my mother was tremendously challenging. She suffered from depression, paranoia, schizophrenia, I wasn't even sure, and I desperately wanted her to be healthy. There wasn't a lot of information on bipolar disorder back then, at least I had not heard of it. Even though there is more awareness now, the stigma associated with mental illness remains.

Eventually, it became easier to spot the warnings when an episode was about to occur. In order to cope, I developed my own mantra – this is not my mother, she is not herself, it's out of her control, just be patient. And when it became too unbearable, I would cut my visit short or end the conversation.

My birth father also reentered my life, and I learned more about what happened between him and mother. Finally, I had an explanation for why he was not around for a huge percentage of my childhood. As the story was told to me, my father had joined the Army, and while away, received word that my mother had moved on and had married someone else. Another lie exposed, another secret revealed, another step towards freedom. I identified with my birth father's heartbreak and began to open up.

By the time I was thirty, I was divorced, working full-time, living on my own, and I discovered I was pregnant. The relationship had already ended, so there was no proud father in the picture. I was hard on myself and felt tremendous guilt and shame at being pregnant and single. But I had also accomplished much. I had graduated from high school and college, and I was financially stable. Three links in the chain shattered!

During one particularly memorable conversation with my dad, I gathered enough courage to ask him if he had other kids--if I had any brothers or sisters. His response was "not that he knew about." But the most significant thing about that conversation was hearing for the first time the words, "I am proud of you." No one until that moment had ever spoken those words to me. He went on to tell me that I had done a great job of raising myself with no help from him. He apologized, and in that instant, I forgave him.

From that day forward, I knew without a doubt that I was and would always be his baby girl.

That conversation prompted the beginning of another shift in my life. There was something powerful in having my dad around. He visited me at the hospital when I gave birth to my son. Another link in the chain broken – my son would know his granddad.

The birth of my precious son was a healing event in my own life. He was truly the glue to mend the broken pieces, and bring clarity to my understanding of my childhood, and the people who surrounded me. From the uncle who pulled me out of bed to put a frozen dinner in the oven to my father finally showing up, the proverbial village stepped in. Finally, I understood that my parents were young, fumbling their way through parenthood. That sentiment resonated immensely when I became a mother.

I am forever thankful that my last conversation with my mother was healthy. I was older, probably in my early forties when I had that conversation with my mother. I was sad, burdened by single parenthood, financial strain and was near a breakdown. The years of being the one everyone called on had finally taken their toll. I feel my mother sensed it. We finally had a mother-daughter conversation, where I could be the child and lean on her for guidance and support. She offered to pay for me to go away for a few days just to get away. She made me promise that I would not do anything to hurt myself. In that moment, I feel she sensed I needed her and she could empathize with what I was dealing with. I needed my mama, and finally, finally, she came through for me. Mama was finally the adult, and I was her child.

Less than a week later, my mama was dead. My younger sister found her unresponsive. I went headlong into denial, anger, and guilt. First, there was a denial that this could be happening, having spoken to her only a few days prior. She had even offered to treat me to a weekend getaway to relax. Maybe she knew the end was near and the trip was her way of mending our relationship. Then there was the anger that she had not stopped smoking, evidenced by the ashtray full of cigarette butts on the table next to where she was last sitting. And lastly, the guilt over time lost during our years of estrangement, and the greater guilt that she died alone. Gone now was any opportunity to mend, to apologize, to say I love you, or to say I forgive you.

While the wounds I suffered from my dysfunctional childhood hurt, the death of my parents, and especially the death of my mother, was earth-shattering. Family members often tell me how much I look like my mother. Proudly, I find myself sounding like my mother, even laughing like her. Despite the grief, pain, and disappointments, I found the strength to forgive those who hurt and abandoned me. But all of the links in the chain will not be broken until I finally forgive the person most worthy of my forgiveness: me.

Even with the greatest support system, pain is real. Grief is real. Depression is real. A closed mouth cannot get fed; neither can a closed mouth ask for help. After years of functioning in survival mode, I am learning that it is okay to ask for help whether from friends, family, even professional help, and merely surviving is not the same as thriving. Being vulnerable and sharing experiences help to build unbreakable bonds and just might offer a glimpse of hope to someone unable to see a way out of their situation.

To that someone, I say: *hold on, don't give up, and always, always give it one more day.*

# A Letter of Hope for my Daughter

*By Nakayla C. Leggett*

*"I see my precious two-year-old girl and try to imagine her at twenty. Sometimes I'm afraid our relationship will become strained or disconnected, especially considering my relationship with my own mother. And so, I write this as a letter to the young woman my daughter will become. I write to explain, and to understand, and to heal."*

Dear Babygirl,

I've seen your secret struggles. I recognize them, because I have secrets, too. There are some scars in mommy's childhood that were not addressed, and so I now write to protect you from that hurt and damage. My hope is that this letter will provide a start to the healing that we both desperately need. Even if you do not know this now, as I write, looking at your precious two year old face, you will one day. I want to share my heart with you.

At three months old I attended my first high school graduation. You guessed it! I was an infant at your grandmother's graduation! Even before she finished high school, she became my mother. I am the product of high school sweethearts.

My childhood is a blur until the 3rd grade. I've always wondered why my 3rd grade was so significant for me. Now I know it was during that year I experienced my first dose of shame and humiliation. As I write this I can feel tears coming at the memory of something so innocent being blown up by mom.

One gloomy day my mother was cleaning out my book bag – you know organization is not mommy's strong suit. She stumbled across a half written letter to a boy in my class. "Dear Jacob, you got the eyes that make a girl want to cry" was all I had written. My mother immediately told her best friend about the letter, and then tacked the letter on the wall in the living room to shame me. And, indeed, I was ashamed, but also angry, and sad, but mostly I felt betrayed. I felt my mother had not only blasted my business to everyone that would listen, but worse, she didn't care about the internal scars she caused me.

After this letter I was sure my mother hated me. I could hear it in her voice. Nothing my mother said to me was nurturing in my eyes. Instead, she was always demanding that I do something, or yelling because I had done something wrong. Third grade ended and it was also my last recollection of getting into trouble at school because I so deeply feared public humiliation.

I was on a new path that I now know was the search for acceptance and approval from my mother. I behaved my best in school and always strived to excel in school, or at least do well. I thought I would surely gain my mom's approval, make her proud, and earn her unconditional love. Unfortunately, that was not the case. It actually felt like the more I excelled the harsher my mom became with her punishment and words.

In the midst of fighting for my mother's approval, social interaction in school became more difficult as I started getting bullied. I remember feeling trapped, because as much as I wanted to tell my mother about the kids at school taking my snack money and calling me names, I was sure she would find a way to flip the script on me as if it was my fault. At school, I suffered in silence. But the more the bullying occurred at school the more angry outbursts I had at home. I remember crying at home often and raising my voice at my mother for her harsh words or punishments that seemed extreme.

One of her harshest punishments occurred twice, first in the seventh grade, and again during my sophomore year of high school. During each of those years, my mother allowed me to try out for cheerleading, and each time, I made the squad. I was so excited! I was part of a team, and I felt special. Cheerleading was beyond a sport to me, it was an outlet that allowed me to feel a sense of accomplishment, and of course gave me the feeling of belonging to something. Then a day came during each of those years when I may have talked back or not cleaned something, or just made my mom mad. I don't even remember what triggered her. As punishment, each time, she made me quit the entire squad. She made me quit something I loved, and made me suffer the hurt and humiliation of publicly quitting my team. Those wounds follow me even today.

I learned never to let my mother see me smile in excitement. It seemed as though if she knew I cared about something, she would snatch it from me as punishment for the slightest level of misbehavior. She used her power over me to take away things I valued. I still have trouble to this day calling my mother and letting her know about an exciting adventure in my life. When I call her with news of accomplishments, I find myself watering down the details so it doesn't feel like a big deal. I'm a grown woman, but that frightened little girl is always there, reacting to protect my inner feelings with an outer shell of protection. I have found that I also do this with other people because I fear they won't be as happy for me as I am. I'm afraid anyone will talk me out of my decision or sabotage my chances.

When my mother was under extreme stress, her blowups would cut so deeply. I remember when a cherished family member passed away. My mother was in her room mourning in privacy. I rarely, if ever, saw my mom cry or express distress in front of anyone, let alone her children, unless it was an angry outburst. I remember standing in the hallway waiting for permission to walk into my mother's room. When I spoke to her, mom yelled back, "I wish it was me instead!" insinuating that instead of that family member dying she wished it had been her. At that moment I felt like a burden to my mother, which was an eerie feeling.

Of course, I would never want my mother to leave this earth especially thinking I was the cause. But her extreme outbursts became so common that I grew numb and accustomed to them. It was easier to tolerate her moods if I created a barricade around my feelings.

I would often find myself in tearful screaming matches with my mother not because I wanted to disobey, but because I just wanted to be heard. My feelings would manifest so big internally that the only place for them to go was out. And because yelling was a form a communication taught early in my home, that is how I, too, responded.

I would never want this pattern of destructive and unpleasant communication to develop between the two of us. So, I write to you hoping to disrupt the family cycle. I know the lens through which I parent you will affect your focus as you transition through life. I would like you to have a sturdy foundation, and a clear outlook.

In my household, silence meant you were good and any words were typically a critique on your faulty process. Words of love and pride were so rarely expressed and stated in my house that I can remember vividly the first time my mother spoke them to me. When I graduated college, I finally heard my mother say, "I am so proud of you and I love you, Baby." This is why my heart lights up each time she hangs up with you or your siblings; she will not end the call without 'goodnight' and 'I love you.' I guess it is true grandchildren bring about change that may have not have been present before.

And I'm glad for it.

As I write this letter to you, Babygirl, I realize the terrible bruises from my mother's physical punishment did not carry over and show up nearly as darkly and boldly as the psychological wounds. As a child, I hated my mother. However, as I reflect back as an adult and a therapist I have a better understanding of her logic. In her mind, if she provided "tough love" so I would not follow in her footsteps. Her main goal was getting her babies out of school without having babies. She succeeded, but only at the expense of my mental stability and especially my self-worth.

I have come to call her method nonfunctional anxious love. Parents typically want their children to do better than they did. They see the faults and mistakes and negative experiences of their own childhood, and encourage the exact opposite. The approach is reactionary and extreme, even if the intention is to be better. I think this is true of my mother. It might even be true of me, Babygirl.

My mother was not a horrible person, and the rest of our needs were always met.

I often saw my mother go without things to provide for us. My mother was also a supportive backbone to many, including family, friends, and even those in her work environment. I believe she was often emotionally depleted, because in her own moments of need I rarely saw others come to her rescue, and I rarely saw her ask for assistance.

Babygirl, your mother also learned this trait. I felt so compelled to give, but I noticed that same level of assistance was rarely reciprocated. I used to blow up with resentment the same way my mother would blow up. How dare they treat me this way! It took self-examination and healing to understand those individuals had learned self- protection and boundaries sooner and better than I had. They took more proper care of themselves first and only offered the overflow to others.

I now get that and have since restructured my faulty view. I understand the importance of self-care and renewal. I have learned boundaries protect sacred spaces, and my love your space is incredibly sacred, so protect it.

I never want you to feel the need to ask, "Mommy why don't you love me?".

When you were first born I knew that raising you would be a challenge. All my childhood pains, and fears, and feelings of inadequacy rushed into my memory when you were about 3 weeks old, and I suffered postpartum depression. I spiraled down all the "what ifs", a parent could have. The most paralyzing of these self-defeating questions was "what if I'm too hard on her and she grows up to hate me?" I had no blueprint for a healthy mother-daugher bond.

I guess you can say I, too, experienced a form of nonfunctional anxious love. I would always pass you over to your father for nurturing because I feared I would fail you. My irrational thoughts about parental failure would be so loud in my own head, I feared a verbal outburst, so I would isolate myself and avoid contact.

Never believe for a second that I don't love you. I loved you so much that I wanted to protect you from inheriting the lingering effects of my childhood pain. My hope is this letter will soothe your heart as much as it has healed my soul to write it.

*Love always, Mom*

## POSTSCRIPT

Sometimes we have to address situations to release them. As a result, I wrote this chapter, this letter to my daughter, through the lens of forgiveness and understanding.

For years I would never touch this topic out loud because I thought I would hurt someone I love dearly. However, I now understand that sometimes the thing most painful to hear may be the very key to healing wholeheartedly. You never know how low your voice is until one day you need it and it doesn't speak up for you. This process is allowing me to do this without hurting someone I love, especially knowing that the hurt was not intentional but cyclical.

With this chapter, I bear witness to yet another graduation. This is the symbolic graduation of that little girl I was in the third grade. She can finally grow up and transition in peace. She is used to watching me and protecting my feelings but I am finding, gradually, that I no longer need her protection. I give her full release of her duties. I'm ready to step outside of my comfort zone, and live.

I'm also grateful that my mother and I have cultivated an amazing relationship that I would have never seen coming as a child. Her harsh words consistently fueled me to excel in my career and seek independence. Understand, though, this level of forgiveness did not happen overnight, and it came with some hard lessons.

First, I learned that just because your pain is not physical or easily seen does not mean that it is insignificant and not detrimental to your wellbeing. In effort to heal from something that goes against what society deems as "real pain" you must dismiss that notion and understand each person is unique. My view of an experience may not be the same as another person's. For a long time, I thought my pain was not sufficient or worthy enough to process aloud, because it was not as harmful as something such as physical abuse. However, I have come to realize that my story is important to be told for both personal healing as well as healing for my generation. Understand that pain is inevitable and if you don't speak up for your pain no one will.

I learned that academic intelligence is not a substitute for emotional intelligence. I used to strive for academic excellence. It got me the degrees, but I had no clue how to genuinely celebrate my accomplishments. As a result, I was always planning and chasing the next accomplishment. As my moments of success multiplied, my unhappiness continued to rise as well. I realized my lack of emotional processing made each achievement less valuable, less meaningful. Taking time to acknowledge, process, and filter emotions is vitally important.

I learned that too much "tough love" can get in the way of natural love. Tough love often relies on fear-based tactics. If a person fears you the person will comply with demands out of fear of repercussions, not because they respect and love you. This does not mean you have to parent without consequences, but just ask yourself, what is the purpose and will my response get me closer to that goal or further away? I ask myself: what kind of love do I want my child to associate with me?

I learned thoughts and words of shame only paralyze the person's voice. We all want those closely connected to us to succeed and excel beyond measure. However, understand that your words mean things. If your child is used to hearing all the things they did wrong in scenarios and rarely the parts they did well in, or always exposing their faults to others in hopes to guilt them into doing better be prepared for a backlash, and a child who fears speaking up.

I have learned to cherish mutual gratitude. When gratitude is expressed mutually it creates love and through this chain, an unbreakable bond is formed. There is power in learning how to outwardly express your gratitude toward others, even when they don't. This creates space for others to see that their appreciation is valued and to reciprocate. And if they don't, you have just cause to remove them from your sacred space.

Lastly, I learned great mothers don't always hit the mark, and that's the human experience. We are all growing imperfectly in different ways, at different paces, and toward different outcomes.

There will always be barriers to success. There will be some things that do not turn out as planned, despite our best efforts and good intentions, and that is okay. We assess the damage, so we can make repairs and keep moving forward. Above all, we must learn to forgive each other, mothers and daughters, grandmothers and granddaughters, and in doing so, forgive ourselves.

> *"Today I am thankful for my history, not because I wanted to go through hardships and pain, but because the lessons gained along my journey have created a healthier vision for my future."* ~ N.C.L.

> *"You can spend a lifetime masking your authenticity to others but that reflection at night will always call your bluff and fight you! So deal with your stuff!"* ~ N.C.L.

# Conclusion:
# Tough Love is Strength Training
*By Alyssa Lowray*

*"Your pain is the breaking of the shell
that encloses your understanding."*

*– Kahlil Gibran*

It has taken me a long time, but I have begun to appreciate the difficult lessons I learned as my mother's daughter. I was an adult before I could see her and appreciate her as a woman handling her own struggles – as an imperfect human being – and not simply as my mother.

One of the hardest truths for me to realize and accept was my mother wasn't perfect. I saw her with a child's eyes, and could not understand how complicated our lives, and our relationship could become. As a child, I thought of her as Wonder Woman, and I believed she could do anything.

Recognizing she was only human was difficult. Dealing with that reality, and accepting her imperfections helped me to understand so much about our relationship as mother and daughter. In accepting and embracing her flaws, I've also learned to love and embrace my imperfections.

My mother was tough on me in several ways, but raising me to be strong was her priority. Every excuse I was never allowed to give to her I can now never make for myself. As mean as I sometimes felt she was, I recognize now she prepared me to push through when the world proved it was even meaner.

Being mad about everything I couldn't have as a child helped me realize as an adult that I had to work for anything I wanted. And acknowledging the things I never had taught me humility. Had I been a spoiled brat, and been given everything, I would have ended up entitled and lazy with no respect for the world that I had no hand in creating.

Instead, I credit my mother with providing me a realistic view of the world--and a broader perspective.

So, I've started to see the blessing in my struggle. What I once called "tough love" I now think of as my strength training. And I have my mother to thank for it.

# Audra Upchurch

*Audra Upchurch* is passionate about helping men and women with a clear vision produce elite, high level book collaborations that elevate their brand and provide a unique, educational and profitable experience to the lead author and contributors. She understands that owning and sharing our individual stories is an important ingredient if we are ever to leave a lasting legacy for those that follow.

Born and raised in Brooklyn, New York, to a mother who suffers with mental illness, and Audra lived in a household that was extremely unstable. As a result, she was homeless by the age of fifteen, a single mother at seventeen, and quickly heading down a dark path, but through prayer and the belief that she deserved more, Audra persevered, graduated college, earned her MBA, and has been able to live her best life.

As a 4x bestselling author, speaker, and entrepreneur Audra helps authors find their voice, shape their stories, and navigate the writing process to deliver a meaningful manuscript.

She is the CEO, of The UPFAM Group, LLC, an organization that captures our philanthropic, mentorship, and community-based activities.

She gives her heart, time, and treasure to support programs that help women, families, and youth who are struggling with mental health issues and homelessness. I believe that life is all about choices, and I thank you for choosing to connect with me!

Feel free to contact me at info@audraupchurch.com, call me at 757-279-8879, and connect with me on all social media outlets at @AuthenticAudra

# Nydia E. Guity

*Nydia E Guity* is a native of the Bronx, New York and identifies as Garifuna. Nydia is a Licensed Clinical Social Worker (LSCW) by profession and co-author of the book, *Black Therapists Rock: A Glimpse Through the Eyes of Experts.*

She is also the creator of www.MsGuity.com – formerly www.yournaturalhairapist.com – a website created for black women to encourage self-confidence and acceptance, overcome emotional barriers, and cultivate natural, outward beauty.

Her own decision to embrace her natural hair in 2007 punctuated her evolving commitment to emotional and physical health, and inspired her mission to encourage other women of color to love their inherent, unique beauty. She credits her own process for her strengthened ability to discern and forgive.

Stay connected with Nydia at www.MsGuity.com.

# Michele Mikki Jones

***Michele Mikki Jones*** is a published author, speaker, poet, and advocate. She holds a B.S. in Social Work from Norfolk State University, and is the founder of *Michele's Visual Imaginations* and *Lupus 365*.

As a speaker and advocate, Michele focuses on healthy living, healing, and self-care. She seeks to empower women with coping skills and techniques that aid in the healing process, and places emphasis on cultivating and protecting healthy relationships.

Michele is active in her community, and maintains memberships in several societies and business organizations.

Learn more about Michele and her work at www.sistaskeeper.com.

# Cynthia Williams-Bey

***Mrs. Cynthia Williams-Bey,*** a native of Brooklyn, New York, is the CEO & Founder of Heaven Sent Childcare, LLC and Spring Forth, LLC. She is a published author and recipient of ACHI Magazine's 2016 Author of the Year Award and has been featured on the podcast *Young Women on a Mission* and on the Instagram page of the PBS Television Network for her work and leadership in her community.

She also serves as Outreach Director for Liberation Church. Williams-Bey, one of nineteen siblings, is married and has five children.

Learn more about her at www.mrswilliamsbey.com

# Winifred A. Winston

*Winifred A. Winston* is a special education school administrator, educator, author, speaker, advocate, and business coach. She is also the founder of Dyslexia Advocation™, which seeks to educate, empower, and equip African-American parents with tools to support their children with dyslexia, dysgraphia, dyscalculia, or other language learning differences. The organization serves populations lacking access to accurate information about dyslexia interventions and instructional strategies.

Additionally, Winifred is a volunteer state leader for a dyslexia grassroots organization, and co-founder of their local advocacy and support group for parents and children in Baltimore City, Maryland.

Connect with Winifred A. Winston on Facebook and LinkedIn, and @winifredwinston on Instagram and Twitter

# Renetta D. Weaver

**_Renetta D. Weaver_** is a Clinical Social Worker, Neuroscience Coach, writer, and speaker with international reach. She has cultivated a clinical focus on interpersonal conflict and forgiveness, borne of her own process and path to sustainable health through significant, permanent weight loss.

Affectionately known as the 'Unstuck Queen,' and the 'First Lady of Integrative Mental Health and Wellness,' she is an adoptee, and childhood trauma survivor.

Connect with Renetta at www.renettaweaver.com.

# Sonia F. James

*Sonia F. James* holds a B.B.A. in Healthcare Management, and has over twenty years of management experience in the healthcare industry. She is also an Independent Beauty Consultant. She is a resident of Virginia, and the proud mother of a college junior. Her contribution to this book is her first foray into writing and publishing, and she readily speaks of the empowerment sharing her story has afforded her.

Reach Sonia by email at MySisterIsMe757@gmail.com.

# Nakayla C. Leggett

*Nakayla C. Leggett* is a Behavioral Wellness Counselor with focused training in trauma modalities, and a public speaker. She is the author of the children's book, *Mama, Why is my Flower Wilting?* and a co-host on 4 Sistahs podcasts, which promotes mental wellness and sisterhood among women of color.

Nakayla earned undergraduate and graduate degrees from Winston-Salem State University and NC State, respectively. She takes a keen interest in the mental and emotional health of the millennial generation and their families.

Nakayla lives in Elizabethtown, NC with her husband – her high school sweetheart – and their two small children.

To connect, email her at nakaylaleggett@gmail.com

CPSIA information can be obtained
at www.ICGtesting.com
Printed in the USA
JSHW020715191219
2952JS00006B/11